500 RECIPES FOR SANDWICHES AND PACKED MEALS

D0658651

500 RECIPES
for Sandwiches and Packed Meals

---

by Catherine Kirkpatrick

Hamlyn
London · New York · Sydney · Toronto

Cover photography by James Jackson
Published by The Hamlyn Publishing Group Limited
London · New York · Sydney · Toronto
Astronaut House, Feltham, Middlesex, England

© Copyright The Hamlyn Publishing Group Limited 1964

All rights reserved. No part of this publication may be reproduced, stored in a retrieval system, or transmitted, in any form or by any means, electronic, mechanical, photocopying, recording or otherwise, without the permission of The Hamlyn Publishing Group Limited.

First published 1964
Reprinted 1984

ISBN 0 600 32405 2
Printed and bound in Great Britain by
R. J. Acford

Contents

Introduction

It was John Montagu, 4th Earl of Sandwich, who invented the dish that we now know as a 'sandwich' nearly 200 years ago. He called for a piece of meat between two slices of bread so that he could eat without leaving the gaming table.

His invention had an effect on the culinary world, only equalled by that of Mrs. Beeton, and one wonders if he would recognise his sandwich in the many varieties that we serve today.

Sandwich making is an art, although if you are faced with preparing them every day for the children to take to school or for your husband's lunch, you probably do not agree. But, when you stop to think about it, is there any meal easier to prepare? It is surprising how many families have one sandwich meal a day, yet how few cookery books cater for this need and supply recipes to cover this important aspect of meal planning.

It is not necessary to be a *Cordon Bleu* to make a good sandwich; it is simply a question of planning real all-purpose food around bread, a basic food in itself. Bread, with butter, margarine, meat, fish, cheese, eggs, salad, fruit, milk, coffee, fruit juice or soup, and you have a well-balanced meal.

Although one is happy to serve sandwiches for any occasion, the packed meal which is prepared at least five days a week requires very careful planning. It must contain a good proportion of the day's nutriments for building and repair as well as providing energy, vitality.

For building and repair we need:

Milk and all kinds of cheese, meat, fish and eggs. Bread is a useful building food too when combined with milk or cheese, etc.

For energy:

Starchy, sugary foods for fuel, and Vitamin B1 to release the energy from these foods.

Foods rich in B1 are liver, pork, ham, bacon, cod's roe, yeast bakery, all breads.

For vitality:

Iron-rich foods which include liver, corned beef, eggs, sardines, curry, cocoa, plain chocolate, all breads.

Vitamin C is also needed for vitality and repair work:
Foods rich in Vitamin C are oranges, lemons, grapefruit, cabbage, tomatoes, blackcurrants, gooseberries, strawberries, orange and tomato juice. Radishes and watercress also contain some Vitamin C.
It is important to choose foods correctly, and to plan packed lunches to make sure all needs are covered.

A seven-point plan for packing complete meals

Bread as a basic energy food

Pack a variety, choose from sliced white and brown, chunks of crisp Vienna and French stick, baps and rolls, fruit and malt breads (good with cheese), caraway and rye (good with smoked fish, meat and cheese).

Plenty of building foods

Milk and cheese are the best. Choose a variety of cheeses—Dutch, Cheshire, Caerphilly, Dunlop, Wensleydale etc. Add more building foods —fish, beef, lamb, eggs, ham, salami.

Iron-rich foods maintain vitality

Hard-boiled eggs, liver paste, corned beef, sardines, gingerbread, chocolate cake.

Vitamin C for repair and vitality

Citrus fruit, salad vegetables.

Something sweet (unless slimming)

Sweet buns, biscuits, cakes, dried fruits.

Something crisp to finish the meal

Apple, raw carrot, radishes, celery.

Don't forget a drink

Fresh fruit juices, tomato juice and milk are most nutritious.

Some Useful Facts and Figures

Comparison of English and American weights and measures

English weights and measures have been used throughout this book. 3 teaspoonfuls equal 1 tablespoon. The average English teacup is ¼ pint or 1 gill. The average English breakfast cup is ½ pint or 2 gills.

When cups are mentioned in recipes they refer to a B.S.I. measuring cup which holds ½ pint or 10 fluid ounces. The B.S.I. standard tablespoon measures 1 fluid ounce.

In case it is wished to translate any of the weights and measures into their American, Canadian or French counterparts, the following tables give a comparison.

Liquid measure

The most important difference to be noted is that the American and Canadian pint is 16 fluid ounces. The American ½-pint measuring cup is therefore actually equivalent to two-fifths of a British pint.

French weights and measures

It is difficult to convert to French measures with absolute accuracy, but 1 oz. is equal to approximately 30 grammes, 2 lb. 3 oz. to 1 kilogramme. For liquid measure, approximately 1¾ English pints may be regarded as equal to 1 litre; 1 demilitre is half a litre; and 1 décilitre is one-tenth of a litre.

Solid measure

English	American
1 lb. Butter or other fat	2 cups
1 lb. Flour	4 cups
1 lb. Granulated or Castor Sugar	2 cups
1 lb. Icing or Confectioners' Sugar	3 cups
1 lb. Brown (moist) Sugar	2½ cups
1 lb. Golden Syrup or Treacle	1 cup
1 lb. Rice	2 cups
1 lb. Dried Fruit	2 cups
1 lb. Chopped Meat (finely packed)	2 cups
1 lb. Lentils or Split Peas	2 cups
1 lb. Coffee (unground)	2½ cups
1 lb. Soft breadcrumbs	4 cups
½ oz. Flour	1 level tablespoon*
1 oz. Flour	1 heaped tablespoon
1 oz. Sugar	1 level tablespoon
½ oz. Butter	1 level tablespoon
1 oz. Golden Syrup or Treacle	1 level tablespoon
1 oz. Jam or Jelly	1 level tablespoon

* must be proper measuring tablespoon

Oven temperatures

DESCRIPTION OF OVEN	APPROXIMATE TEMPERATURE CENTRE OF OVEN °F.	THERMOSTAT SETTING
Very Slow or Very Cool	200–250 250–300	¼=240 ½=265 1=290
Slow or Cool or Very Moderate	300–350	2=310 3=335
Moderate	350–375	4=350
Moderately Hot to Hot	375–400	5=375 6=400
Hot to Very Hot	425–450	7=425
Very Hot	450–500	8=450 9=470

Types of Bread

Think of a sandwich and the mind instantly turns to a combination of bread and butter plus a filling. If sandwiches form an important part of your meal planning for the week, it is worth taking some trouble with the choice of bread. These are some of the types available:

White breads from unenriched dough

Tin loaf
This everyday bread may be unwrapped or wrapped, unsliced, or sliced in three different thicknesses, and is useful for sandwiches and toast.

Sandwich loaf
Has a flat top giving even, square slices and may be white or brown. A small loaf gives 10-12 slices, a large loaf, 20-24 slices.

Pistol or rasp
Baked in a cylindrical, corrugated tin for even slicing. Is also called 'landlady's' or 'lodger' loaf.

Crusty white bread

Coburg
A dome shaped loaf baked on oven bottom, and may have a pattern of slashes on top.

Cottage
A traditional, hand-made bread, baked on the oven bottom.

French stick
Long thin baton, with or without poppy seeds. at its best a few hours after baking. To serve, cut diagonally or break.

Vienna breads
Large variety of shapes—horseshoe, winkle, baton. It has a thin crisp crust and tender, white crumb.

Poppy seed plait
Very crusty plaited loaf profusely decorated with poppy seeds.

White breads from enriched dough

Farmhouse
A popular loaf, enriched with fat, with a lengthwise slash and floury top. It is sometimes wrapped and sliced.

Flat loaves
This type of loaf is known by traditional names in different regions, e.g. Scotch bap, Irish bap, Devon flat, Essex paddle. It is enriched with varying quantities of lard and sugar, is oval or round in shape and has a floury top.

Milk loaves
Variety of shapes, including winkles, batons, square, oval and rounds. Enriched with milk and usually glazed.

Cholla
A rich plaited Jewish bread, glazed and topped with poppy seeds. Egg, fat and sugar give it a soft yellow crumb. It keeps well and toasts well.

Bloomer
Long loaf with rounded ends. The top is slashed several times before baking so that the loaf can 'bloom' up or rise better.

American
Soft crusted, tin baked loaf which toasts and keeps well. It is usually wrapped and sliced.

Brown breads

Wholemeal
A true wholemeal is made from flour from the entire wheat grain. It has a close texture and a good nutty flavour. The loaves are often sprinkled with cracked wheat and may be shaped as cobs, pots and batons.

Stoneground Wholemeal Bread
The flour for this type of loaf is ground between stones instead of metal rollers. It has the same nutritive value as wholemeal bread.

Wheatmeal bread

Tin or cob shaped, made from a mixture of white and wholemeal flour, and is lighter in texture than wholemeal.

Wheatgerm bread

Tin shape, made from white or brown flour with wheatgerm added. It is usually sold under proprietary names.

Proprietary breads

These are breads made from special recipes and flours and are sold under brand names.

Malt
Granary, Bermaline
Wheatgerm
Hovis, Vitbe, Daren, Turog
Special Meals
Allisons, Brownie, Scofa
Starch Reduced
Nimble, Nutrex, Procea, Slimcea
High Protein
Energen

Rye breads

There is a wide variety of shapes, varying from the very heavy dark Russian rye to a light caraway kummel.

Rolls and buns

Rolls are as variable as breads

Crusty white

Many shapes—batons, coils, crescents, knots, Kaise rolls, Vienna rolls

Soft white

Bridge rolls, small baps, tea cakes, hamburger rolls, finger rolls, muffins.

Brown

Wholemeal, wheatmeal, wheatgerm, proprietary rolls

Rich rolls

Croissants, brioches, Aberdeen butteries

Types of Sandwiches

Lunch pack

2 slices of bread or a halved roll spread with butter and put together with a filling.

Open

A slice of bread spread with butter and covered with a colourful combination of different foods.

Toasted

Slices of bread, enclosing a moist filling. The complete sandwich is toasted under the grill and served hot. Usually eaten with a knife and fork.

Fried

Prepared the same way as a toasted sandwich but fried in shallow or deep oil.

Hot

Slices of bread or toast topped with fish, meat, etc. covered with a sauce and eaten with a knife and fork.

Double-decker or Club

Three or more slices of bread or toast, spread with butter and put together with different fillings in each layer.

Tea-time

Made from thinly-sliced bread, may be sweet or savoury, or cut with fancy cutters. The crusts are usually removed.

Canapés

Very small open sandwiches, bread or toast, cut into fancy shapes, spread with butter, covered with thinly sliced meat, etc. usually glazed with aspic jelly and garnished. Served as an appetiser.

Choose the Right Bread

BREAD should be chosen to suit the sandwich and the fillings.

FOR CLOSED SANDWICHES sliced white and brown loaves are quick and convenient. Unsliced breads such as Farmhouse, Bloomer, Milk, Wholemeal, Wheatgerm, Malt and Fruit breads, should be used to add variety of flavour and texture. For slicing the bread, a good bread knife with a scalloped (not saw-toothed) edge is a necessity. To cut thin slices easily, use bread one day old or store in the refrigerator for a few hours before cutting.

FOR OPEN SANDWICHES use a loaf with a firm crisp crust which will keep each slice in shape, e.g. French, Vienna, wholemeal, or rye caraway breads.

BUTTER, or margarine, can be permanently softened by beating 1 dessertspoonful of hot water in to each 4 oz. butter. A 'spreadable' butter or margarine is very important because this 'waterproofs' the slice of bread and prevents the filling soaking in. For spreading, a small palette knife is useful.

Hints on Sandwich-making

Prepare spreads and soft fillings beforehand and keep in a cool place.

Slice meats or cheese and wrap in foil or polythene bag until ready for use.

Hard-boil eggs in advance. They keep several days in a cool place. Wash and drain green vegetables and keep ready for use in a polythene bag.

Bread may be buttered ahead of time. Put slices with buttered sides facing and put together again as a loaf. Keep in a polythene bag until ready for use.

Many ingredients may be chopped or sliced beforehand if they are kept cool and crisp and not allowed to dry out.

Storage
When making sandwiches the night before, do not use sliced tomatoes, cucumber, beetroot or lettuce, as these will soak into the bread. Sandwiches containing these items should always be prepared as freshly as possible.

Sandwiches may be kept moist by wrapping in a damp cloth and then in aluminium foil, waxed paper, polythene bags or greaseproof paper. Keep in a refrigerator or cool place until needed.

Wrap each type of sandwich separately so the flavours of the various fillings do not mix.

Quantities

A large loaf gives 20-24 slices.
A small loaf gives 10-12 slices.

Allow:
4 oz. creamed butter for 10-12 sandwiches
1 oz. creamed butter for 3 bread rolls
Approximately 8 oz. cold meat for 9 large sandwiches.

Fillings

Be adventurous when you are preparing sandwiches—add a few sliced maraschino cherries to blue cheese, flavour mayonnaise with curry powder to add to an egg sandwich, tuck a few chopped, cooked prunes into a pork sandwich and you will be surprised at how easy it is to earn the reputation of being a good cook.

Uncooked

Two or more of these fillings can be used to make double-decker or club sandwiches. They can be toasted or fried or open sandwiches like the Scandinavian Smørrebrød. They can be made with white, brown, or rye bread, or with any of the crispbreads available.

Here are some suggestions:

MEAT

Minced lamb with chopped mint.

Minced beef with horseradish cream.

Minced chicken with minced ham and finely chopped pineapple.

Minced chicken with chopped celery and chopped walnuts.

Thin slices of pork spread with thin slices of apple or spread with apple sauce.

Corned beef, flaked and mixed with a little chopped chutney.

Luncheon meat, chopped and mixed with chopped stoned prunes and chopped olives.

FISH

Smoked haddock, or other fish, mixed with a little parsley sauce.

Salmon with chopped cucumber and a little mayonnaise (see page 79).

Tuna with chopped gherkin and tomato, bound with mayonnaise (see page 79).

White fish with a little anchovy essence or chopped shrimps.

Sardines with lemon juice and chopped cucumber or watercress.

EGGS

Hard-boiled eggs

If a soft creamy filling is required, mash eggs while still warm and if butter is one of the other ingredients, it mixes more easily with the warm egg.

Hard-boiled egg, chopped and mixed with tomato sauce and chopped gherkin.

Scrambled eggs (see page 84) with chopped chives or parsley.

Scrambled egg with chopped fried bacon or chopped cooked sausage.

Scrambled egg with chopped cooked mushrooms and chopped watercress.

CREAM CHEESE VARIATIONS

It is generally best to beat the cheese with a wooden spoon until smooth and creamy, then add the other ingredients.

The following suggested additions can be used in proportions according to your own taste. A little cream or milk can always be added if necessary to soften the filling.

Cream cheese with chopped olives, chopped celery and seasoning to taste.

Cream cheese with chopped green pepper, pimento and walnuts.

Cream cheese with chopped dates and raisins.

Cream cheese covered with thin slices of tomato and sprinkled with very finely chopped onion or chives.

Cream cheese, chopped watercress, little horseradish cream makes a good filling for brown bread.

Cream cheese with chopped fillets of anchovy and a dash of cayenne pepper.

Cream cheese with chopped watercress and a little finely chopped luncheon meat or corned beef.

Cream cheese with grated orange rind, chopped walnuts and raisins.

Cream cheese with drained chopped pineapple.

GRATED CHEESE

3 oz. grated cheese mixed with 1 oz. butter, seasonings, salt, pepper and ½ teaspoon made mustard and moistened with about 1 tablespoon beer.

The beer omitted from the above recipe and 1 tablespoon cream and a little chopped watercress added.

Grated cheese mixed with sauce tartare (see page 78) and covered with thin slices of cucumber.

Grated cheese mixed with grated raw carrot, finely chopped chives, salt and a dash of cayenne pepper, bound with a little sour cream or mayonnaise (see page 79).

Grated cheese with chopped apple and walnuts.

Grated cheese with chutney, chopped gherkins and capers.

SLICED AND PROCESSED CHEESE

Slice of cheese, spread lightly with chutney and topped with a slice of luncheon meat.

Slice of cheese, spread lightly with a little vegetable or meat extract and topped with scrambled egg (see page 84).

Slice of cheese covered with chopped celery and apple bound with a little salad cream (see page 79).

Two thin slices of cheese with thinly sliced beetroot in the centre.

Note

When beetroot is used in a sandwich it should be eaten as soon as possible after the sandwich is made.

Processed cheese with scrambled egg (see page 84).

Processed cheese with tomato slices and chopped chives.

Egg and shrimp

you will need:

3 hard-boiled eggs
knob butter
seasoning
3 - 4 tablespoons shrimps, canned or frozen
2 - 3 stuffed olives
lemon juice or vinegar (optional)

1. Peel and mash the eggs while still warm. Add the butter and seasoning.
2. Add shrimps and chopped olives, correct seasoning.
3. A few drops of lemon juice or vinegar might be considered an improvement.

Egg and beetroot

you will need:

2 hard-boiled eggs
2 small cooked beetroots (about 8 oz.)
1 tablespoon finely chopped onion
1 teaspoon vinegar
salt, pepper
1 teaspoon horseradish sauce (see page 78)
3 - 4 tablespoons sour cream or yoghourt

1. Chop eggs and beetroot very finely.
2. Mix together.
3. Add onion, vinegar, seasoning and horseradish sauce.
4. Add enough sour cream or yoghourt to bind.

Note

This makes a very appetising sandwich filling but is not suitable for a packed lunch as the beetroot is inclined to spoil the colour if it is left for any length of time.

Egg and anchovy

you will need:

3 hard-boiled eggs
¼ oz. butter
1 dessertspoon anchovy essence
squeeze lemon juice
pepper

1. Chop eggs while still warm and mash well with butter.
2. Add anchovy essence, lemon juice and pepper to taste.

Hard-boiled egg and tomato

you will need:

3 hard-boiled eggs
¼ oz. butter
1 tablespoon tomato ketchup
1 teaspoon chopped capers
seasoning

1. Chop eggs while still warm and mash with butter.
2. Add tomato ketchup, capers and seasoning.

Egg and sausage

you will need:

3 hard-boiled eggs
salt and pepper
2 cooked sausages
little French mustard

1 Slice eggs and sprinkle with salt and pepper.
2 Skin the sausages, slice thinly and arrange on the egg.
3 Spread lightly with French mustard before completing the sandwich.

Egg and ham

you will need:

3 hard-boiled eggs
pepper and salt
3 oz. chopped cooked ham
salad cream (see page 79)

1 Chop eggs and add pepper and salt.
2 Add ham and just enough salad cream to bind.

Variation

To the above ingredients add 2 oz. chopped celery and 6 chopped olives.

Egg and liver

you will need:

2 hard-boiled eggs
4 oz. cooked liver
little French dressing (see page 80)
seasoning
squeeze garlic juice (optional)

1 Chop eggs and liver very finely.
2 Mix together and moisten with the French dressing.
3 Add seasoning as required and garlic juice if used.

Egg and bacon

you will need:

1 tablespoon mayonnaise (see page 79)
1 tablespoon French dressing (see page 80)
1 teaspoon lemon juice
3 hard-boiled eggs, chopped
2 oz. chopped cooked bacon
4 chopped olives
seasoning

1 Mix mayonnaise, French dressing and lemon juice together.
2 Add eggs, bacon and olives.
3 Add seasoning as required.

Egg and vegetable

you will need:

2 hard-boiled eggs
2 oz. cucumber, chopped
2 oz. celery, chopped
½ small red pepper, chopped
1 teaspoon chopped chives
tomato purée
1 - 2 tablespoons mayonnaise (see page 79)

1 Chop eggs and add cucumber, celery, red pepper and chives.
2 Add just enough tomato purée to the mayonnaise to flavour it and to give a pale pink colour, then use to bind all other ingredients together.

Egg and cheese

you will need:

4 oz. cream cheese
1 teaspoon chopped chives
3 hard-boiled eggs
salt and pepper

1 Mash cheese and add chives.
2 Spread on buttered bread and arrange slices of egg on top.
3 Sprinkle with salt and pepper and complete the sandwich.

Devilled egg and ham

you will need:

3 hard-boiled eggs
2 oz. chopped cooked ham
1 tablespoon chilli sauce (see page 78)
½ teaspoon made mustard
1 teaspoon Worcestershire sauce
little mayonnaise (see page 79)

1 Chop eggs finely and mix with ham.
2 Add other ingredients and just enough mayonnaise to make a moist filling.

Crab and cucumber

you will need:

1 3½ - 4 oz. can crab
3 - 4 oz. cucumber
mayonnaise (see page 79)
salt and pepper
mustard and cress

1 Remove all the small bones from the crab and flake finely.
2 Add cucumber, peeled and finely chopped.
3 Add enough mayonnaise to bind and season carefully.
4 Spread one slice of buttered bread with this mixture, sprinkle with mustard and cress and complete the sandwich.

Sardine and egg

you will need:

1 can sardines
1 hard-boiled egg
½ teaspoon Worcestershire sauce
1 dessertspoon salad cream (see page 79)
1 stick celery, chopped
salt and pepper

1. Remove tails and backbones from sardines, then mash.
2. Chop egg.
3. Mix all ingredients together thoroughly.

Salmon

you will need:

1 7 - 8 oz. can salmon
mayonnaise or salad cream (see page 79)
lemon juice or vinegar to taste
salt and pepper

1. Remove bone and any black skin from salmon and mash well.
2. Add enough mayonnaise or salad cream to bind, lemon juice or vinegar to taste and season carefully.

Variations

1. Add 1 - 2 tablespoons chopped gherkins.
2. Add 1 tablespoon chopped capers.
3. Add 2 - 3 tablespoons finely chopped cucumber.
4. Omit the lemon juice or vinegar and add 1 tablespoon horseradish cream (see page 78) and a little grated cheese.

Cod's roe

you will need:

4 - 6 oz. cooked cod's roe
½ teaspoon celery salt
1 oz. watercress, finely chopped
mayonnaise or salad cream (see page 79)
seasoning
lemon juice or vinegar (optional)

1. Chop the roe finely.
2. Add celery salt and watercress.
3. Add enough mayonnaise to bind, then correct the seasoning.
4. You may find a little lemon juice or vinegar will be an improvement; much depends on the mayonnaise.

Tuna and tomato

you will need:

1 small can tuna
2 tomatoes
1 oz. watercress
mayonnaise (see page 79)
salt and pepper
vinegar

1. Flake and mash fish well.
2. Peel and chop tomatoes.
3. Chop watercress.
4. Mix ingredients together and add enough mayonnaise to bind.
5. Add seasoning and vinegar to taste.

Tuna and capers

you will need:

1 4 - 4½ oz. can tuna
1 tablespoon chopped capers
½ teaspoon paprika
3 tablespoons mayonnaise (see page 79)
lemon juice
salt

1. Drain oil from fish, and mash well.
2. Add capers and paprika.
3. Moisten with mayonnaise, add lemon juice and salt to taste.

Variations

1. Omit the paprika and add 1 tablespoon chopped canned pimento.
2. Substitute 1 tablespoon tomato ketchup for mayonnaise.

Fish and tomato

you will need:

8 oz. cooked white fish
2 - 3 oz. shredded cabbage heart
2 tomatoes
parsley sauce (see page 78) or mayonnaise (see page 79)
seasoning
lemon juice

1. Flake fish finely, removing any skin and bones.
2. Add cabbage.
3. Peel, seed and chop tomatoes and mix with fish and cabbage.
4. Add enough parsley sauce to make a moist filling.
5. Add seasoning and lemon juice to taste.

Creamed haddock

you will need:

- 8 oz. cooked smoked haddock
- 3 tablespoons cream
- 1 tablespoon chopped parsley
- salt
- freshly ground black pepper
- lemon juice

1. Flake fish finely.
2. Add cream, parsley, seasoning and lemon juice.
3. Mix all well together.

Sardine and celery

you will need:

- 1 can sardines
- 2 hard-boiled egg yolks
- 1 teaspoon anchovy essence
- 2 teaspoons anchovy paste
- 2 oz. butter
- freshly ground black pepper
- lemon juice

1. Remove tails and backbones from sardines.
2. Put into a fairly large basin with the egg yolks, anchovy essence and paste, and butter.
3. Pound all very well together.
4. Add pepper and lemon juice to taste.

Potted meat

you will need:

- 8 oz. cooked meat
- 2 oz. fat cooked ham
- pepper and salt
- 1 level teaspoon mixed spice
- 2 teaspoons made mustard
- 2 oz. butter

1. Remove any gristle from the meats, cut into pieces and put twice through a mincer.
2. Put the meat into a basin, or into a mortar if available, add seasoning and flavouring.
3. Melt the butter, add most of it to the meat and pound all well together.
4. Press tightly into a jar and cover with the remaining butter.

Note

This will keep for 2 - 3 days in the refrigerator.

Cooked fillings

Mock crab

cooking time 10 – 15 minutes

you will need:

- 2 oz. butter
- 1 small onion, finely chopped
- 8 oz. tomatoes
- 1 egg, beaten
- 2 - 3 oz. grated cheese
- salt and pepper
- ¼ teaspoon made mustard
- breadcrumbs from brown loaf

1. Heat butter, and sauté the onion until it is soft but not coloured.
2. Peel, seed and chop tomatoes and cook for about 10 minutes.
3. Cool a little, add the egg, then return to the heat and cook for a few minutes over gentle heat.
4. Remove from the heat, add cheese, seasoning and mustard.
5. Add sufficient breadcrumbs to make a spreadable paste.

Cheese and tomato

cooking time 5 – 10 minutes

you will need:

- 1 oz. butter
- 2 large tomatoes, peeled and chopped
- 4 oz. grated cheese
- 3 oz. breadcrumbs
- 1 egg, beaten
- salt and pepper
- ¼ teaspoon made mustard

1. Heat the butter, add tomatoes and cook for about 5 minutes.
2. Add cheese and breadcrumbs and mix well.
3. Add egg and stir all well togeher over gentle heat.
4. Season carefully and allow to get quite cold before using.

Note

This filling will keep for 2 - 3 days if pressed into a small jar and covered with melted mutton fat or butter.

Scrambled egg and kidney

you will need:

3 eggs
2 tablespoons thin cream or evaporated milk
1 sheep's kidney, grilled and chopped
salt and pepper
½ oz. pepper

1 Beat the eggs slightly, and add the cream, kidney and seasoning.
2 Heat the butter, add the egg mixture and cook slowly, stirring as mixture thickens.
3 Leave to get cold before using.

Liver paste

cooking time about 1 hour

you will need:

12 oz. liver
1 tablespoon cornflour
1 oz. dripping or butter
1 small onion, peeled and sliced
½ pint stock or water
salt and pepper
bouquet garni
butter

1 Cut the liver into thin slices and coat with cornflour.
2 Heat the dripping or butter and fry the liver lightly.
3 Add the onion, cook for a few minutes then stir in the remaining cornflour and mix well.
4 Add the stock and stir till boiling.
5 Add seasoning and *bouquet garni*, cover and simmer very gently for about 1 hour.
6 Remove the liver, put it through a mincer and then rub through a sieve.
7 Add enough of the strained stock to make a soft paste, and correct the seasoning.
8 Press tightly into a basin and cover with melted butter.

Note

This will keep for 2 days in the refrigerator. In addition to using the liver paste as a sandwich spread, it would make a good *hors d'oeuvre* served with toast and butter.

Mushroom

cooking time about 5 minutes

you will need:

6 oz. mushrooms
½ oz. butter
1 tablespoon milk
salt and pepper

1 Wash the mushrooms and drain well, then chop very finely.
2 Melt the butter in a small pan, add the milk.
3 Add the mushrooms and seasoning.
4 Cover and simmer for about 5 minutes stirring occasionally.
5 Drain off any excess liquid and leave to cool before using.

Mushroom and ham

cooking time about 10 minutes

you will need:

4 oz. mushrooms
3 - 4 tablespoons milk
salt and pepper
extra milk
single cream (optional)
½ oz. butter
½ oz. cornflour
1 egg yolk
2 oz. finely chopped cooked ham

1 Wash, drain and chop the mushrooms.
2 Cook them in the milk with a little seasoning.
3 Strain off the liquid and make it up to ¼ pint with milk or a little single cream and milk.
4 Melt the butter, add the cornflour and mix well.
5 Add the milk, stir till boiling and boil for a few minutes.
6 Remove from the heat.
7 Add the egg yolk, mushrooms and ham and correct the seasoning.

Egg and tomato

cooking time 7 – 10 minutes

you will need:

2 eggs
2 tablespoons milk
salt and pepper
½ oz. butter
2 tomatoes

1 Beat the eggs, add the milk and seasoning.
2 Melt the butter, add the eggs and scramble lightly.
3 Peel, seed and chop the tomatoes and mix with the egg.

Variations

1 Add a little chopped parsley.
2 Add 1 oz. grated cheese.
3 Add 1 teaspoon chopped capers or gherkin.
4 Add 2 teaspoons finely chopped pickle.
5 Omit the tomato and add some flaked cooked fish and a little chopped parsley.

Haddock and egg

cooking time 5 – 10 minutes

you will need:

4 oz. cooked smoked haddock	little made mustard
3 eggs	1 tablespoon water
pepper and salt	little lemon juice
	1 oz. butter

1 Flake the fish finely and be sure it is free of bones.
2 Beat eggs with seasoning and a little made mustard.
3 Add fish, water and lemon juice to taste.
4 Melt the butter, add the fish and egg mixture and cook like scrambled egg (see page 84).
5 Leave to get cold before using.

Sausage scramble

cooking time 5 – 10 minutes

you will need:

3 cooked sausages	little made mustard
3 eggs	1 tablespoons water
salt and pepper	½ oz. butter

1 Skin the sausages and chop finely.
2 Beat the eggs, add seasoning, a little mustard and the water.
3 Stir the sausage into the egg mixture.
4 Heat the butter, pour in the mixture and scramble in the ordinary way.
5 Allow to get cold before using.

Simple Spreads

Although the use of butter is purely functional since it 'waterproofs' the bread, it can be used to add an interesting flavour which lifts the sandwich into the extra special class.

For example, a flavoured butter can be made by adding 1 tablespoon of lemon juice and 1 teaspoon of grated lemon rind to ¼ lb. salt-free butter, or omit lemon rind and add ½ tablespoon finely chopped chives or water-cress. 1 tablespoon table mustard or 2 table-spoons drained prepared horseradish can also be added to the butter to give an interesting taste.

If a quantity of sandwiches has to be made and time is the important factor, the butter may be blended with the filling so that only one spreading operation is required.
In this case, the ingredients for the filling should be chopped, grated or shredded.

No special equipment is needed to make Spreads. Ingredients can be chopped, mashed or minced to a spreadable consistency. It is very important to make sure that the spreads have a good flavour. Have some cubes of bread ready for tasting.

The following recipes are all made from a basic spread to which different ingredients can be added. The mix can be made in large quantities and kept ready for up to 2 weeks in a refrigerator. This is an easy way to make a variety of spreads from one basic mix.

Basic spread mix

2 oz. butter or margarine	2 heaped teaspoons soya flour* or ground almonds
1 dessertspoon boiling water	

* Soya flour can be bought at health food stores and some grocers.

1 Cream butter or margarine.
2 Add hot water and soya flour or ground almonds and beat well.

With this basic mix, you can make the following spreads, each of which should be sufficient to cover 6 - 8 slices of bread.

Cheese spread

4 oz. grated cheese (mild Cheddar)	pepper to taste
1 tablespoon milk	1 tablespoon chopped gherkins
squeeze lemon or vinegar	or 1 tablespoon chopped olives, chives or onions

Add to the basic mix and work in.

Blue cheese spread

1 - 2 oz. Danish blue cheese
2 - 3 oz. grated Cheddar cheese
1 tablespoon milk
1 teaspoon vinegar

Add to the basic mix and work in.

Curry spread

2 - 3 tablespoons curry powder or paste
2 teaspoons peanut butter
1 teaspoon meat or yeast extract
½ teaspoon sugar
rind and juice ½ lemon

Add to the basic mix and work in.

Egg and anchovy spread

2 chopped hard-boiled eggs
2 teaspoons anchovy essence or chopped anchovies
pepper to taste

Add to the basic mix and work in.

Crunchy peanut spread

2 oz. salted peanuts, roughly chopped
2 heaped tablespoons peanut butter
1 saltspoon meat extract

Add to the basic mix and work in.

Chocolate spread

2 - 3 tablespoons cocoa powder
1 dessertspoon black treacle
2 dessertspoons condensed milk
2 dessertspoons boiling water
vanilla or grated orange rind, or drop peppermint, or rum

1 Beat first four ingredients well.
2 Add flavouring.
3 Add to basic mix and work in.

These recipes do not use the basic mix

Savoury cheese and bean spread

1 can baked beans in tomato sauce
2 - 3 oz. grated cheese
pepper

1 Mash the baked beans with the cheese.
2 Make into a smooth paste.
3 Season with pepper.

Horseradish spread

you will need:

2 oz. butter
1 dessertspoon boiling water
1 - 2 teaspoons horseradish relish

Cream butter, work in water and relish.

This spread is excellent with beef, corned beef or tongue sandwiches.

Kipper spread

2 raw kipper fillets skinned or 1 kipper skinned and boned
1 heaped tablespoon breadcrumbs
1 oz. margarine
squeeze lemon juice
pinch grated lemon rind
pinch pepper
curry powder

1 Mince or chop kipper and add breadcrumbs.
2 Mix to a smooth paste with margarine and lemon juice.
3 Season to taste with lemon rind, pepper and curry powder.

Liver spread

8 oz. ox liver
1 oz. butter or margarine
1 oz. flour
pinch pepper
scant ½ pint milk
2 teaspoons anchovy essence or paste (optional)

1 Cut liver into small pieces and fry lightly in fat for 3 minutes.
2 Remove liver and mince it.
3 Add flour, pepper, milk, and anchovy essence to the pan and make a thick sauce.
4 Mix with minced liver to make a paste.

Corned beef spread

2 oz. butter
2 oz. corned beef, chopped
1½ oz. grated cheese
1 teaspoon curry powder
1 teaspoon Marmite
1 tablespoon tomato purée
cayenne

1 Make a paste with creamed butter corned beef and cheese.
2 Blend in rest of ingredients and season to taste with cayenne.

Open Sandwiches and Rolls

A Scandinavian speciality

An open sandwich is made of 1 slice of bread, well buttered, with ingredients arranged so the bread is completely covered. The ingredients should look attractive and be combined for good flavour. Open sandwiches may be served as party food or for a light lunch or supper. They can be eaten with a knife and fork.

Combine 2 or more of the following:

Open sandwiches on round slices of crusty white bread

slice liver paste
fried bacon curls and mushrooms

corned beef or luncheon meat
sliced pickled beetroot

soused herring
chopped onion
Pimento strip

slices pilchards
chopped radishes
raw egg yolk

Open sandwiches on wholemeal bread

sardines
lettuce
lemon twist
tomato wedges

lettuce
hard-boiled egg
mayonnaise
shrimps

slice cold roast pork
fried apple and onion

dressed crab
sliced cucumber

Open sandwiches on rye bread

rectangle of bread with row of tomato slices on one side, egg slices on the other, mayonnaise and chopped chives down the centre

cream cheese or cottage cheese with rolls or twists of salami, chopped beetroot

slice of cooked pork, topped with thin slice unpeeled orange and a few cooked stoned prunes

slices of cold roast beef, chopped raw leeks or onion rings and sandwich spread in the centre

Use crisp pieces of lettuce or whole leaves for decoration or base.

Salmon rolls

you will need for 4 servings:

1 small can salmon
4 oz. cooked green peas
salt and pepper
lemon juice
1 small can evaporated milk
4 large soft bread rolls
butter
4 thin slices cheese

1 Flake the fish and put into a pan with the peas, seasoning, lemon juice and milk.
2 Stir over a gentle heat until smooth and creamy.
3 Split the rolls, spread lightly with butter and cover with a cheese slice.
4 Pile mixture on top and cover with other half of the roll.

Stuffed rolls

cooking time 10 – 15 minutes

you will need for 4 servings:

4 baps or breakfast rolls
melted butter or corn oil
4 eggs
2 tablespoons milk
salt and pepper
2 oz. cheese, finely grated
4 teaspoons tomato ketchup

1 Cut the top off each bap or roll and scoop out the centre. Use this for making a stuffing or in place of breadcrumbs in a meat mixture.
2 Brush shells and lids with butter or corn oil and put into a moderate oven (350°F.—Gas Mark 4) or under a grill until lightly toasted.
3 Scramble the eggs (see page 84), remove from heat when almost set.
4 Sprinkle the inside of each roll with grated cheese, fill with scrambled egg.
5 Put 1 teaspoon tomato ketchup in centre of each. Replace lid.
6 Bake in a moderate oven (350°F.—Gas Mark 4) for 5 minutes.

Double-decker or Club Sandwiches

Feeling hungry? Just think of the number of good ingredients that can be packed between slices of bread to give you a nourishing meal in no time. Whether you like bread as it comes or prefer it toasted or fried, there is no end to its versatility as the basis of a good square meal.

Niçoise

you will need for 1 sandwich:

2 tablespoons tuna
2 anchovy fillets, chopped
mayonnaise (see page 79)
seasoning
3 slices buttered bread
1 hard-boiled egg
2 - 3 radishes
2 black olives (optional)
1 tomato
1 teaspoon chopped chives

1. Flake and mash the fish and mix with the chopped anchovy fillets.
2. Moisten with a little mayonnaise and check the seasoning.
3. Spread this on first slice of bread and cover with the second.
4. Arrange sliced hard-boiled egg, sliced radishes and tomato on top and olives, if used.
5. Cover with third slice of buttered bread.

Salmon and cucumber

you will need for 1 sandwich:

1 small can salmon
salad cream or mayonnaise (see page 79)
3 slices buttered bread
cucumber
salt and pepper
vinegar

1. Flake and mash the salmon and moisten with a little mayonnaise.
2. Spread on the first slice of bread and cover with the second.
3. Slice the cucumber thinly, sprinkle with salt and pepper and add a little vinegar.
4. Allow to stand for about 10 minutes, then drain, and arrange on the second slice of bread.
5. Cover with the third slice.

Ham and egg

you will need for 1 sandwich:

little made mustard
chopped cooked ham or bacon
3 slices buttered bread
seasoning
scrambled egg (see page 84)
chopped parsley

1. Mix a little mustard with the ham or bacon and arrange on 1 slice of bread.
2. Thoroughly season the scrambled egg.
3. Add a little chopped parsley and spread on the second slice of bread.
4. Cover with the third slice of bread.

Ham and pineapple

you will need for 1 sandwich:

mustard
chopped cooked ham, or canned pork luncheon meat
3 slices buttered bread
canned pineapple
cream cheese
walnuts, chopped

1. Mix a little made mustard with the finely chopped ham and spread on 1 slice of bread.
2. Chop the pineapple finely and mix with a little cream cheese and walnuts.
3. Spread this on the second slice of bread.
4. Cover with the third piece of bread.

Egg and cheese

you will need for 1 sandwich:

1 hard-boiled egg
3 slices buttered bread
seasoning
cream cheese
little chopped celery
little grated or finely chopped apple

1. Slice the egg and arrange on the first slice of buttered bread.
2. Sprinkle with salt and pepper, and cover with the second slice.
3. Mix the cream cheese with the celery and apple, add salt to taste and use as the second layer. Cover with remaining slice.

Variation

A little grated raw carrot can be substituted for the celery.

Ham with egg and mushrooms

thinly sliced ham or luncheon meat
3 slices buttered bread
made mustard
1 hard-boiled egg
2 oz. cooked mushrooms, chopped
salt and pepper
little sour cream or mayonnaise (see page 79)

1 Put a good layer of ham on 1 slice of bread and spread lightly with mustard.
2 Cover with the second slice of bread.
3 Chop the egg and add the chopped mushrooms.
4 Add seasoning and bind with the cream or mayonnaise.
5 Complete the sandwich as usual.

Corned beef, egg and cabbage

you will need for 1 sandwich:

1 slice corned beef
3 slices buttered bread
1 hard-boiled egg
seasoning
¼ firm cabbage heart
2 - 3 drops chilli sauce (see page 78)
1 teaspoon chopped pickles
1 tablespoon mayonnaise (see page 79)

1 Put a good slice of corned beef on 1 round of buttered bread.
2 Cover with slices of egg and sprinkle lightly with salt and pepper.
3 Cover with the second slice of bread.
4 Shred the cabbage very finely.
5 Add the chilli sauce and pickles to the mayonnaise and mix with the cabbage.
6 Spread this on the second slice of bread and cover with the third.

Lamb and celery

you will need for 1 sandwich:

slices cooked lamb
3 slices buttered bread
redcurrant jelly
1 stick celery, chopped
3 tablespoons finely chopped almonds
mayonnaise (see page 79)

1 Arrange slices of lamb on 1 slice of buttered bread and spread lightly with the redcurrant jelly.
2 Cover with the second slice.
3 Bind the celery and almonds with a little mayonnaise and use as the second layer.
4 Cover with the third slice of buttered bread.

Chicken and cheese

you will need for 1 sandwich:

slices cold cooked chicken
2 - 3 fried bacon rashers
3 slices buttered bread
2 oz. blue cheese
1 - 2 stuffed olives

1 Arrange the chicken and bacon on 1 slice of buttered bread and cover with the second.
2 Mash the cheese, add the stuffed olives and use as the second layer.
3 Cover with the third slice of bread.

Cheese and tomato

cooking time 6 minutes

you will need for 1 sandwich:

3 slices bread
butter
4 oz. cheese, grated
1 tablespoon milk
1 level teaspoon made mustard
2 firm tomatoes
salt and pepper
castor sugar
lettuce or watercress

1 Lightly toast the bread on one side only.
2 Butter untoasted sides.
3 Blend cheese, milk and mustard to a paste and spread over the buttered sides of the toast.
4 Slice tomatoes, arrange on cheese mixture.
5 Sprinkle tomatoes with salt, pepper and sugar.
6 Cook under a medium grill until cheese browns and sizzles.
7 Pile slices of bread on top of each other, cheese sides up.
8 Press lightly together, cut into triangles and serve at once, accompanied by lettuce or watercress.

Variations

Cheese and pineapple

Prepare as above, omitting tomato, and top each cheese slice with well-drained chopped pineapple.

Cheese and bacon

Prepare toast and cheese mixture as above, omit tomatoes. Top each cheese slice with 1 back rasher cut in half.
Grill until bacon is cooked and cheese melted.
Serve as above.

Tongue and Swiss cheese

you will need for 1 sandwich:

slices tongue
3 slices buttered bread
little made mustard
thin slices gherkin
1 slice Swiss cheese
thin slices radish

1. Put slices of tongue on the first slice of buttered bread. Spread lightly with mustard and add gherkin.
2. Cover with the second slice of bread and put cheese on top.
3. Arrange radish on top of the cheese and cover with the third slice of buttered bread.

Processed cheese

cooking time about 5 minutes

you will need for 1 sandwich:

3 slices toast
little made mustard
3 slices processed cheese
little sweet pickle, chopped

1. Spread 2 slices of toast with a little mustard.
2. Put 1 slice of cheese on top of each and grill for 2 minutes.
3. Pile one on the other, cheese side up, cover with remaining toast, spread with a little sweet pickle and then cover with the last slice of cheese.
4. Grill for a few minutes.

Toasted Sandwiches

Bacon and cheese

cooking time about 5 minutes

you will need for 1 sandwich:

butter
2 slices bread
2 rashers bacon, cooked
1 thin slice cheese

1. Butter 1 side of each slice of bread.
2. Flatten bacon until quite thin.
3. Put bacon on 1 slice of bread, cover with the cheese, then press on the other slice of bread.
4. Toast on both sides.

Corned beef and tomato

cooking time about 5 minutes

you will need for 1 sandwich:

1 slice corned beef
2 slices buttered toast
little horseradish cream or mustard
1 tomato, peeled and sliced
salt and pepper
1 tablespoon grated cheese

1. Put corned beef on 1 slice of toast and spread with horseradish cream or mustard.
2. Add tomato, peeled and sliced, and sprinkle with a little salt and pepper.
3. Cover with remaining toast.
4. Sprinkle cheese on top and brown lightly under the grill.

Bacon and banana

cooking time about 10 minutes

you will need for 1 sandwich:

2 slices bread
little butter
pinch curry powder
2 rashers streaky bacon
1 banana, sliced lengthwise
1 slice processed cheese

1. Toast both pieces of bread on one side only.
2. Spread the untoasted side with butter to which curry powder has been added.
3. Arrange bacon on top alternately with the banana. Put under the grill to cook the bacon.
4. Cover with the second slice of bread — the untoasted side downward.
5. Place cheese on top and grill until the cheese begins to brown.
6. Serve at once.

Barbecue bean

cooking time 10 minutes

you will need for 4 sandwiches:

- 8 slices white bread
- 1 8 oz. can cooked beans in tomato sauce
- 1 tablespoon horseradish sauce (see page 78)
- 1 teaspoon made mustard
- 4 streaky bacon rashers, cooked crisp
- 4 slices Cheddar cheese
- paprika
- green salad

1. Toast bread on one side.
2. Cover 4 slices, on toasted sides, with beans blended with horseradish, mustard and crumbled bacon pieces.
3. Top with remaining bread, toasted sides down.
4. Toast one side and turn.
5. Top with cheese and grill until cheese is melting.
6. Sprinkle with paprika and serve at once with green salad.

Egg and mushroom specials

cooking time 10 minutes

you will need for 4 sandwiches:

- 8 slices bread
- 4 hard-boiled eggs
- 2 - 4 freshly cooked mushrooms
- seasoning
- 2 tablespoons mayonnaise (see page 79) or soured cream
- salad garnish

1. Very lightly toast bread on one side.
2. Finely chop eggs and mushrooms, blend with mayonnaise and season to taste.
3. Warm mixture and spread over 4 of the toasted sides and top with remaining bread, toasted sides down.
4. Toast both sides and serve at once with salad garnish.

Devilled pâté sandwiches

cooking time 5 minutes

you will need for 4 sandwiches:

- 8 slices bread
- 4 oz. liver paste or liver sausage
- 1 tablespoon finely chopped onion
- 1 tablespoon tomato ketchup
- ½ level teaspoon dry mustard
- ½ teaspoon Worcestershire sauce
- 2 rashers bacon, halved and grilled

1. Lightly toast bread on one side.
2. Mix liver paste, onion, ketchup and seasoning and spread over toasted side of 4 slices.
3. Top each with grilled bacon, then with remaining bread, toasted sides down.
4. Toast both remaining sides, garnish with crisp salad. Serve at once.

Variation

Rich Devilled Pâté

Follow the recipe as above, adding 1 crushed clove of garlic and 1 teaspoon dry sherry with the ketchup and seasoning.

Grilled Sandwiches

Sweet and sour tuna

cooking time 5 minutes

you will need for 4 sandwiches:

4 slices bread
butter
1 7 oz. can tuna
2 - 3 tablespoons mayonnaise (see page 79)
4 pineapple rings
4 slices Cheddar cheese

1 Toast bread on one side only, lightly butter untoasted side.
2 Flake tuna, chop roughly and mix with mayonnaise.
3 Spread tuna mixture on buttered sides, top each slice with pineapple ring, well drained.
4 Cover with a slice of cheese.
5 Grill until cheese is melted.
6 Serve hot.

Danish

cooking time 10 minutes

you will need for 4 sandwiches:

4 slices bread
2 oz. mushrooms, sliced
1 oz. butter
4 oz. cheese, finely grated
1 egg, lightly beaten
salt and pepper
1 tomato
sprigs watercress

1 Toast bread on one side only.
2 Sauté mushrooms in butter, over a gentle heat, for 5 minutes.
3 Stir in grated cheese and egg.
4 Add seasoning to taste, blend mixture together with a wooden spoon and spread on untoasted slices of bread.
5 Grill until cheese melts.
6 Serve garnished with a slice of tomato and sprigs of watercress.

Eggs Créole

cooking time 10 minutes

you will need for 4 sandwiches:

4 slices bread
butter
1 can sweetcorn
4 eggs
2 oz. cheese, grated
4 tomatoes, sliced

1 Toast bread on one side only.
2 Spread untoasted side with butter.
3 Meanwhile, heat sweetcorn.
4 Poach eggs in salted water (see page 85), drain well.
5 Top each slice of bread with sweetcorn, place 1 egg on top of each and sprinkle with grated cheese.
6 Put under a hot grill for 2 minutes.
7 Serve accompanied by slices of tomato.

Variation
Omit grated cheese and serve with cheese sauce (see page 78) poured over each slice.

Dutch

Prepare as for Eggs Créole, using baked beans in tomato sauce in place of corn. A little finely chopped onion may be cooked with the beans for added flavour.

Sweet Sandwiches

Sandwiches made with sweet bread and/or sweet fillings are really desserts and should not be used in place of substantial meat or other protein food sandwiches. Some are suitable for tea, ideal for a children's tea party or to be served instead of cake or biscuits with a snack meal or in a packed meal. Cut these sandwiches into finger lengths.

Home-made sweet breads are excellent for making these sandwiches, and you will find easy recipes for these on pages 73 - 76.

Spread bread, rolls or scones with butter and top with one of the following:

chopped drained apricots, sprinkled with chopped almonds or desiccated coconut.

grated plain chocolate mixed with grated dessert apple.

mashed banana blended with honey, sprinkled with cinnamon.

cream cheese with blackcurrant jam.

raspberry jam and canned peach slices, well drained.

raisins soaked in orange juice blended with honey.

lemon curd and thin slices of orange (peel removed).

grated dessert apple sprinkled with lemon juice, blended with honey.

chocolate spread (see page 20) mixed with chopped walnuts and raisins.

crushed pineapple and sliced bananas sprinkled with lemon juice.

lemon curd with plain chocolate, coarsely grated.

Dessert sandwiches

The following fillings are based on a cream cheese mixture.
To fill 8 sandwiches, blend 8 oz. cream cheese with 3 tablespoons butter, work in ½ cup of one of the following:

canned raspberries, well drained and mashed with a fork.

canned plums, well drained and mashed with a fork.

canned mandarin oranges, well drained and chopped.

canned peaches, well drained and chopped.

mashed banana, sprinkled with lemon juice, mixed with marmalade.

mincemeat mixed with 1 chopped dessert apple.

cooked prunes, chopped and mixed with stewed apple.

dates, chopped and mixed with chopped peeled orange, chopped nuts and raisins.

Snacks

Do not be depressed at the thought of a snack meal. It does not have to be baked beans on toast and even if it does you can make this old standby more interesting by adding a few fried onion rings or grilled bacon or a sprinkling of grated cheese. Put it under the grill for five minutes and you have a tasty snack.

The dictionary definition of a snack is a slight or casual meal, and if this is what you have in mind, soup and a sandwich will make an excellent combination. By taking care in the choice of soup just as you do with the choice of bread, you can add interest and variety to the snacks that you serve. Mushroom or chicken soup is an ideal partner for a chicken sandwich, vegetable soup is good with cheese, green pea soup with ham. You have probably discovered how good and convenient packet and canned soups are, but if you still prefer to make your own and have the time, you will find recipes on pages 66 - 68.

Fried

Cheese slices

cooking time 5 – 10 minutes

you will need for 2 sandwiches:

4 ½-inch thick large slices stale bread
little milk
2 eggs
4 oz. grated cheese
salt and pepper
cayenne pepper
butter

1 Put bread into a shallow dish. Cover with milk and leave for a few minutes, then drain.
2 Beat eggs, add cheese and seasoning.
3 Spread this on the bread, then put into a frying pan, cheese side down, and fry in butter until hot and crisp.

Cheese dreams

cooking time 3 – 4 minutes

you will need for 1 sandwich:

butter
2 slices bread cut from large loaf
horseradish cream (see page 78)
1 slice processed cheese

1 Butter each slice of bread, spread lightly with a little horseradish cream and make a sandwich with the cheese.
2 Press well, remove crusts and cut diagonally in half.
3 Fry the sandwich in butter, on both sides, until crisp and golden.

Ham and pineapple

cooking time 5 – 7 minutes

you will need for 1 sandwich:

2 tablespoons finely chopped or minced ham
2 tablespoons crushed or finely chopped pineapple
little French mustard
2 slices buttered bread
½ egg
2 tablespoons milk
salt and pepper

1 Mix ham and pineapple together and add mustard.
2 Spread on 1 piece of bread and cover with the other.
3 Beat egg with milk and add seasoning.
4 Dip sandwich in egg mixture and fry in butter until crisp and golden on both sides.

Chicken

cooking time about 10 minutes

you will need for 1 sandwich:

2 oz. minced cooked chicken
1 dessertspoon finely chopped celery
1 dessertspoon chopped apple
little mayonnaise (see page 79) or salad cream
salt and pepper
2 slices bread
½ egg
1 tablespoon milk
butter

1 Mix chicken, celery and apple together.
2 Bind with mayonnaise. Add seasoning as required.
3 Sandwich between the bread, pressing well together.
4 Dip in egg and milk and fry in butter until well browned.

Ham toasties

cooking time 8 minutes

you will need for 2 sandwiches:

4 slices bread
butter
½ level teaspoon made mustard
2 thin slices ham or cooked bacon
2 eggs
4 tablespoons milk
½ teaspoon salt
corn oil

1 Spread 4 slices bread with butter mixed with a little mustard.
2 Cover 2 slices with ham, sandwich together with the remaining bread. Press firmly together.
3 Beat eggs together with milk and salt.
4 Dip sandwiches in egg mixture moistening each side well.
5 Fry gently in hot oil until golden.
6 Drain on kitchen paper and serve.

French toast

cooking time 10 minutes

you will need for 4 sandwiches:

2 eggs
4 tablespoons milk
½ teaspoon salt
good pinch pepper
4 slices bread
corn oil
4 bacon rashers
4 - 8 apple rings

1 In a soup plate beat the eggs in milk. Add seasoning.
2 Remove crusts from bread. Soak 1 slice at a time in egg mixture until thoroughly moistened.
3 Remove from mixture and fry until golden on both sides.

4 Place on a plate and keep hot while remaining slices are being fried.
5 Fry or grill bacon rashers and apple rings.
6 Serve each slice topped with bacon and 1 or 2 apple rings.

Sweet French toast

Prepare as 1 to 4 above, omitting pepper.
5 Serve sprinkled with brown sugar and cinnamon, accompanied by stewed fruit.

Varied

Chicken and pineapple

cooking time 1 – 2 minutes

you will need for 4 servings:

2 - 3 oz. cream cheese
little made mustard
dash lemon juice or vinegar
3 - 4 oz. chopped cooked chicken
2 rings pineapple, chopped
4 slices buttered toast

1 Mix the cheese, mustard, lemon juice, chicken and ¾ of the pineapple, season to taste.
2 Pile on to hot buttered toast, decorate with remaining pineapple and grill for 1 - 2 minutes.

Scotch eggs

cooking time about 10 minutes

you will need for 4 servings:

4 hard-boiled eggs
2 tablespoons flour
12 oz. sausage meat
1 egg
3 - 4 tablespoons milk
breadcrumbs

1 Shell the eggs and coat lightly with flour.
2 Divide the sausage meat into 4 portions, and cover each egg as evenly as possible with it.
3 Beat the egg, add milk, then coat each wrapped egg carefully with the egg mixture and breadcrumbs.
4 Fry in deep fat, allowing time for the sausage meat to cook well.

Scotch woodcock

cooking time about 5 minutes

you will need for 4 servings:

1½ oz. butter
6 eggs
salt and pepper
2 tablespoons milk
4 slices buttered toast
1 can anchovy fillets
few capers or 1 - 2 sliced gherkins

1 Melt the butter.
2 Add the eggs, beaten slightly, with milk and seasoning.
3 Cook over a gentle heat until the egg becomes creamy.
4 Pile on to the toast and arrange anchovy fillets criss-cross on top.
5 Garnish with capers or sliced gherkins.

French bread pizzaburgers

cooking time 10 minutes

you will need for 4 servings:

1 long French loaf
1 lb. minced steak
1 tablespoon finely chopped onion
2 tablespoons sharp grated Cheddar cheese
½ teaspoon oregano or other favourite herb
2 tablespoons tomato ketchup or purée
extra grated cheese or anchovy fillets

1 Cut bread in half lengthwise, then into 3-inch chunks.
2 Blend steak, onion, cheese and seasonings; spread over bread.
3 Grill fairly slowly until meat is cooked, about 7 minutes.
4 Top each with tomato purée and cook 2 minutes longer.
5 Top each with grated cheese or anchovy fillet.
6 Serve at once, open or sandwiched in pairs, with salad.

Kippered eggs

cooking time 5 – 6 minutes

you will need for 4 servings:

6 - 8 oz. cooked kipper
4 eggs
salt and pepper
1 tablespoon water
1 oz. butter
4 slices buttered toast
little chopped tarragon or parsley

1 Flake the fish and remove bones.
2 Beat the eggs lightly, add seasoning, water and the fish.
3 Melt the butter, add the egg mixture and stir until creamy.
4 Pile on to the toast and sprinkle with tarragon or parsley.

Devilled kidneys on toast

cooking time about 20 minutes

you will need for 4 servings:

- 1 onion, peeled and chopped
- 2 tomatoes, peeled and chopped
- 2 oz. butter
- 2 teaspoons curry powder
- 1 level tablespoon cornflour
- ½ pint stock
- 1 tablespoon chutney
- salt and pepper
- lemon juice
- 12 oz. ox kidney or 6 lamb's kidneys, skinned and chopped
- 4 slices buttered toast

1 Fry the onion and tomatoes in butter until soft.
2 Add curry powder and cornflour and mix well.
3 Add the stock, stir until boiling and boil for 3 minutes stirring all the time.
4 Add chutney, seasoning, lemon juice and kidney.
5 Cook over a low heat until tender, then serve on the toast.

Savoury fish toast

cooking time 10 – 15 minutes

you will need for 4 servings:

- about 1½ lb. cooked smoked haddock or white fish
- salt and pepper
- cayenne pepper
- 1 tablespoon capers, chopped
- 1 tablespoon chopped parsley
- little vinegar or lemon juice
- pinch curry powder
- 2 - 3 tablespoons parsley or anchovy sauce
- 4 slices toast
- browned breadcrumbs
- butter

1 Flake fish finely. Add all the flavourings and seasonings and bind with a little sauce or a little milk or beaten egg.
2 Pile fish mixture on toast, sprinkle with breadcrumbs, dot with butter and put into a hot oven (400°F.—Gas Mark 6) to heat through.
3 Serve with green salad.

Creamed cheese on toast

cooking time 7 – 10 minutes

you will need for 4 servings:

- ¾ oz. cornflour
- ¾ pint milk
- salt and pepper
- 6 oz. grated cheese
- 2 eggs
- 3 tablespoons cream or top of milk
- 3 - 4 chopped gherkins
- 4 slices hot buttered toast

1 Mix cornflour smoothly with a little of the milk.
2 Heat remainder of the milk.
3 Add mixed cornflour, stir until boiling and boil for 1 minute. Add seasonings.
4 Remove from the heat, add the cheese and the beaten eggs.
5 Cook a few minutes without boiling.
6 Add the cream or top of the milk and the gherkins, correct seasoning and pile on to toast.

Egg and sausage cakes

cooking time about 15 minutes

you will need for 4 servings:

- 8 oz. sausage meat
- little minced onion
- black pepper
- pinch nutmeg
- flour
- fat or oil for frying
- 4 eggs

1 Mix sausage meat with the onion, pepper and nutmeg.
2 Divide into 4 and shape each into a round flat cake.
3 Coat with flour and fry on both sides.
4 Meanwhile, poach the eggs (see page 85) and serve 1 on each sausage cake.
5 Grilled tomatoes can be served with this dish.

Spaghetti eggs

cooking time 6 – 8 minutes

you will need for 4 servings:

- 4 slices bread
- butter
- 4 eggs
- 1 large can spaghetti in tomato sauce
- 4 slices cheese

1 Toast bread, butter lightly and keep hot.
2 Poach eggs (see page 85).
3 Heat spaghetti.
4 Place 1 cheese slice on each slice of bread, cover with spaghetti.
5 Top each with a poached egg and serve.

Variation

Slices of cheese can be omitted and the spaghetti can be sprinkled with cheese, grilled until golden brown and then topped with an egg.

Informal Entertaining

A 'sandwich board' is an excellent way of preparing informal meals. You will need a tray of open sandwiches and a supply of buttered bread. Provide a variety of bread for extra interest, as well as a selection of salad ingredients and 'nibbles', olives, gherkins, radishes, sticks of celery, etc.

Small eaters will be happy with an open sandwich accompanied by something to crunch. The more hearty eaters will want to take the sandwich with another slice of bread and those who are really hungry will put a slice of bread between two open sandwiches.

Or, for a change, you might let your guests each compose a sandwich to suit his own taste and appetite. Provide a variety of bread and rolls, butter and raw ingredients for sandwich fillings, pickles, relishes, etc., a good supply of knives then let everyone enjoy a 'do it yourself' party.

Cheese and fruit, followed by coffee, completes the meal, but if the budget allows it, some wine will make the party go with a swing.

Pinwheels

Use a fresh, uncut sandwich loaf. Remove crusts. Cut loaf horizontally into thin slices. Put each slice on a damp cloth (to keep moist and prevent cracking) and spread with creamed butter. Cover with selected soft fillings. Roll up like a Swiss roll. Wrap and chill. Cut into thin slices.

Rolled sandwiches

Remove crusts from slices of very fresh white or brown sandwich loaves. Spread with creamed butter. Cover with a selected filling. Alternatively, place a strip of banana sprinkled with lemon juice or a length of asparagus at one side of each slice. Roll up. Secure each with a cocktail stick and chill. Remove sticks before serving.

Cornucopias

Remove crusts from slices of white or brown bread cut thinly from 24-hours-old sandwich loaves. Cut each slice into a fan shape. Spread with creamy filling. Roll into cones and fasten each with a cocktail stick. Chill. Before serving, remove sticks and garnish to taste.

Fancy shapes

Make sandwiches in the usual way, using thin slices of white or brown bread. Cut into crescents, stars, hearts, etc., with biscuit cutters; or into triangles, fingers, diamonds and squares with a sharp knife.

Ribbon sandwiches

Allow 1 slice white bread to 2 slices brown bread or vice versa. Put the 3 slices together with the odd slice in the centre and with selected soft fillings between the layers. Wrap, chill, cut into 1-inch wedges.

Neapolitan sandwiches

Prepare thin bread and butter, both brown and white, and 3 or 4 savoury fillings of contrasting colours, e.g. tomato, liver pâté, watercress and egg. Spread a piece of the bread and butter with one of the fillings and cover with a second piece of bread, buttered side down. Now butter the top, spread with one of the other fillings and cover with a third piece of bread and butter.

Continue in this way, building up a large block of alternate layers of bread, butter and filling, working the different colours in rotation. Cut off the crusts and press well.

Wrap the whole block in foil or waxed paper and leave in a cool place for some hours with a weight on top. When required, cut into slices across the filling, making sandwiches of many-coloured stripes. Arrange on a plate to show the striped effect.

Devilled cheese and ham sandwiches

you will need for 4 sandwiches:

8 oz. Cheddar cheese	2 - 3 tablespoons mayonnaise (see page 79)
1 teaspoon Worcestershire sauce	8 slices bread
1 teaspoon tomato ketchup	4 slices ham
½ teaspoon dry mustard	butter

1 Grate cheese, add sauce, ketchup and mustard.
2 Blend to a paste with mayonnaise.
3 Spread on to 4 slices lightly buttered bread.
4 Top each with 1 slice of ham.
5 Cover with another slice of bread, press lightly together and serve.

Sophisticated sandwich suggestions

Spread slices of bread with a mixture of butter and blue cheese, in equal quantities. Top with slices of cold roast beef. Sprinkle with finely chopped chives.

* * *

Mix equal quantities of chopped Swiss cheese and chopped walnuts. Season to taste with salt and cayenne pepper. Moisten with enough mayonnaise or salad cream to make a spreading consistency. Spread on wholemeal or rye bread.

* * *

Drain and flake the contents of 1 can tuna. Mix with 2 - 3 tablespoons finely chopped celery adding a good squeeze of lemon juice. Flavour mayonnaise or salad cream to taste with curry powder. Mix together tuna, celery mixture and mayonnaise. Pile on lightly buttered toast and sprinkle with coconut. Or grill until lightly browned.

Assorted canapés

Cut thin brown bread into fancy shapes and on these arrange: asparagus tips, smoked salmon, salami etc. or pipe with a savoury butter (see page 77). Make some aspic jelly according to instructions on packet, and spoon this over the canapés when the jelly is on the point of setting. Garnish with piped savoury butter, pieces of red pepper, etc.

Simple canapés

Lightly spread savoury biscuits with butter and top with one of the following:

Cottage or **cream cheese** mixed with drained chopped pineapple and decorated with a sprig watercress.

Peanut butter topped with a piece of thinly-sliced eating apple and sprinkled well with lemon juice.

Chopped hard-boiled egg mixed with mayonnaise, decorated with sliced stuffed olives or capers.

Crab paste sprinkled with a few drops lemon juice and decorated with a thin slice of cucumber.

Liver sausage topped with a little finely chopped onion or chutney.

Cottage or **cream cheese** decorated with thin slices of preserved ginger.

Grated raw apple sprinkled with lemon juice and mixed with honey.

Processed cheese cut in thin rounds decorated with lattice of drained anchovy fillets.

Sardines mashed with a little or lemon juice decorated with a twist of lemon.

Ham, roughly chopped, and raisins, bound together with mayonnaise.

Grated cheese mixed with chutney or sweet pickle topped with small rolls of cooked bacon or ham.

Apple sauce spread thinly, topped with small pieces of crisply fried bacon.

Cream or **cottage cheese** topped by a mandarin segment or maraschino cherry.

Crab meat moistened with tomato purée decorated with a lemon butterfly.

Grated cheese mixed with mayonnaise and topped with a pickled walnut, or radish rose.

Stuffed celery sticks

Cut sticks of celery into even sized lengths and fill the centre of each with one of the following mixtures:

Minced chicken and cream sauce.

Cream cheese and chopped nuts.

Grated apple, chopped dates and walnuts.

Sieved hard-boiled egg, butter and chutney.

Chopped, cooked bacon and ham with a piquant sauce.

Cheese straws

1 Roll out some cheese pastry (see page 81) thinly and cut into fingers, about 3-inches long and ¼ inch wide. Stamp out a few pastry rings, using 2 inch cutters, and bake in a hot oven (400°F.—Gas Mark 6) for about 10 minutes.
2 When cold, thread the straws through the rings.

Garlic bread

cooking time about 15 minutes

you will need:

1 long French loaf or Vienna loaf	1 clove garlic
	2 oz. butter

1 Cut the bread into slanting slices, not cutting right to the bottom of the loaf.
2 Chop the garlic very finely, or put into a garlic press, and mix well with the butter.
3 Spread the butter on each slice and then press together to re-form the shape of the loaf.
4 Wrap in aluminium foil, leaving the ends open and put into a moderate oven for about 15 minutes (375°F.—Gas Mark 4).
5 Serve with main course or salad meals.

Bacon sandwich

you will need:

2 - 3 rashers bacon
buttered bread

Fry the bacon and when cold arrange between slices of bread.

Variations

1 Add 1 - 2 finely chopped onions.
2 Add 1 - 2 peeled and thinly sliced tomatoes.
3 Add a little grated cheese and grated apple mixed together.
4 Add 1 pickled walnut, finely chopped and mixed with a little grated cheese.
5 Spread lightly with mustard and sprinkle with a little minced or very finely chopped cooked liver.

Beef sandwiches

When using beef for sandwiches it should be sliced thinly or minced and any gristle removed.

Variations

1 Minced meat, mixed with horseradish cream and a little chopped chives.
2 Thin slices of beef, spread lightly with a little French mustard, with a few thinly sliced gherkins.
3 Thin slices of beef, spread lightly with French mustard, sprinkled with finely chopped pickled walnuts.
4 Minced meat, with a little chopped chutney and grated cheese.

Turkey and celery

you will need:

cold cooked turkey
chestnut purée or chestnut cream
chopped celery
mayonnaise or salad cream (see page 79)
seasoning

1 Mince or chop the turkey finely.
2 Add a little chestnut purée and some chopped celery.
3 Add enough mayonnaise or salad cream to make a spreadable mixture.
4 Season carefully.

Note

Chestnut purée or cream is obtainable in tubes, but if unavailable, these sandwiches are very good if the bread is first spread with devilled butter (see page 77).

Tongue and egg

you will need:

6 oz. tongue
2 hard-boiled eggs
salt and pepper
pinch curry powder
salad cream (see page 79)

1 Chop the tongue and the eggs finely.
2 Add seasoning and curry powder and enough salad cream to make a moist filling.

Pork and watercress

you will need:

cold cooked pork
chopped watercress
yoghourt or sour cream
seasoning

1 Chop the pork and add some watercress.
2 Add enough yoghourt to moisten and season as required.

Pork and apple

you will need for 1 sandwich:

cold cooked pork
2 slices buttered bread
1 crisp apple
chopped celery
pinch salt
mayonnaise (see page 79)

1 Cut the pork into thin slices and arrange on 1 slice buttered bread.
2 Peel and chop the apple and mix with some chopped celery. Add the salt and bind with mayonnaise.
3 Spread this over the pork and complete the sandwich.

Corned beef and cheese

you will need:

6 oz. corned beef
2 oz. grated cheese
1 tablespoon tomato or apple chutney
seasoning

1 Flake the corned beef and add the cheese and chutney.
2 Add salt and pepper as required.

Variation

Omit the cheese and chutney and add a little horseradish cream and chopped gherkin.

Pork and ham

you will need:

1 slice cold roast pork
2 slices buttered bread
apple or redcurrant jelly
1 slice cooked ham

1 Put 1 slice of pork on to 1 slice buttered bread.
2 Spread with a thin layer of jelly.
3 Cover with 1 slice of ham and complete the sandwich.

Boiled beef with tomato and anchovy

you will need for 1 sandwich:

1 slice cold boiled beef
2 slices buttered brown bread
tomatoes
pinch sugar
1 - 2 anchovy fillets

1 Put 1 slice of beef on 1 slice buttered bread.
2 Peel and thinly slice the tomato.
3 Cover the beef with tomato and add the sugar.
4 Arrange 1 - 2 fillets anchovy on top and complete the sandwich.

Chicken and almond

you will need:

6 oz. cooked chicken
1½ oz. almonds
cream or mayonnaise (see page 79)
salt and pepper
grated nutmeg

1 Mince or chop chicken finely.
2 Add finely chopped almonds.
3 Add enough cream or mayonnaise to bind.
4 Season and add nutmeg to taste.

Variation

Use 4 oz. chicken and 2 oz. ham or tongue.

Devilled sausage

you will need for 1 sandwich:

2 slices bread
devilled butter (see page 77)
cold cooked sausage or salami
gherkins
capers

1 Spread the bread with the devilled butter.
2 Arrange thin slices of sausage or salami on top.
3 Chop some gherkins and capers and sprinkle on the sausage.
4 Complete the sandwich.

Lamb and cheese

you will need for 1 sandwich:

- 2 slices buttered bread
- redcurrant jelly or mint jelly
- slices cold cooked lamb
- cottage cheese

1. Spread 1 slice of buttered bread sparingly with redcurrant or mint jelly.
2. Arrange slices of lamb on top.
3. Spread cottage cheese on the meat and complete the sandwich.

Lamb and apple

you will need:

- 6 oz. cold cooked lamb
- 1 small dessert apple
- 1 teaspoon grated onion
- ½ teaspoon chopped mint
- mayonnaise (see page 79)
- seasoning

1. Chop or mince the lamb finely.
2. Peel, core and finely chop apple.
3. Mix meat, apple, onion and mint together and add enough mayonnaise to bind.
4. Add seasoning as required.

Patties and Pies

A sweet or savoury pie is always a very acceptable item in a packed meal and, if made on an aluminium foil dish, presents no problem in transport. It is very important to allow the pastry to become really cold before it is packed and always avoid a filling that is too moist, since this will soak into the pastry and spoil it.

Recipes for all pastries are given later in this book but if the picnic is a spur of the moment idea, do not forget the prepared frozen pastries which give such excellent results.

Veal and ham pie

cooking time about 2 hours

you will need for 4 servings:

- 12 oz. hot water crust (see page 82)
- 1 lb. fillet veal
- 8 oz. ham
- salt and pepper
- grated rind ½ small lemon
- 2 hard-boiled eggs
- stock or water
- beaten egg
- 1 level teaspoon gelatine
- ½ level teaspoon meat extract

1. Line a 6-inch cake tin with about ¾ pastry and keep the rest warm.
2. Trim the veal and ham and cut into small pieces. Sprinkle with salt, pepper and lemon rind and put half of it into prepared tin.
3. Cover with slices of egg and add remaining meat and 3 - 4 tablespoons meat stock.
4. Turn top edge of the pastry over the meat and damp it.
5. Roll out remaining pastry into a round and put on top.
6. Press edges very well together and flute with thumb and finger.
7. Brush over with egg, make a hole in the centre and decorate as liked with leaves of the remaining pastry.
8. Bake about 2 hours in a moderate oven (375°F.—Gas Mark 4).
9. Remove from the oven and leave to cool.
10. Dissolve the gelatine in ⅛ pint stock and add the meat extract. Leave until begins to thicken, then pour into pie through the hole in the top.
11. Leave to get quite cold before using.

Tomato and cheese pasties

cooking time — about 30 minutes

you will need:

- 8 oz. rough puff pastry (see page 81)
- 3 tomatoes, peeled, seeded and chopped
- 1 medium-sized onion, peeled and grated
- 2 tablespoons bread-crumbs
- 3 oz. grated cheese
- salt and pepper
- milk

1 Roll the pastry into a square, about ¼ inch thick, and cut into 8 equal portions.
2 Mix all the other ingredients well together, and season carefully.
3 Divide the mixture equally between the pastry pieces, damp the edges, and fold over to form triangles.
4 Knock up the edges of pastry pieces and make slits in the tops.
5 Brush over with milk and bake for 10 minutes in a fairly hot oven (425°F.—Gas Mark 6), then reduce to 375°F.—Gas Mark 4 for a further 20 minutes.

Savoury flan

cooking time — about 40 minutes

you will need:

- 6 oz. lean bacon, chopped
- 1 medium-sized onion, peeled and chopped
- 1 8-inch baked flan case (see page 80)
- 8 oz. cooked potatoes
- 3 eggs, beaten
- 1 level dessertspoon chopped parsley
- salt and pepper

1 Cook bacon and onion together over low heat until onion is beginning to soften, then put into pastry case.
2 Sieve potatoes, add the eggs, parsley and seasoning and pour into pastry case.
3 Bake in a moderate oven about 40 minutes (375°F.—Gas Mark 4).

Sausage, egg and tomato pie

cooking time — 50 minutes – 1 hour

you will need:

- 8 oz. short crust pastry (see page 80)
- 8 oz. sausage meat
- 2 – 3 tomatoes, peeled and sliced
- 2 hard-boiled eggs, sliced
- milk

1 Line an 8-inch pie plate with about ⅔ pastry.
2 Spread with the sausage meat and cover with tomato and egg slices.
3 Cover with the remaining pastry, press the edges well together and flute with the thumb and finger.
4 Score once or twice on the top and brush over with milk.
5 Bake for 10 minutes in a fairly hot oven (425°F.—Gas Mark 6) then reduce to 350°F.—Gas Mark 3. Continue cooking for a further 45 - 50 minutes.

Onion and cheese turnovers

cooking time — 25 – 30 minutes

you will need:

- 8 oz. short crust pastry (see page 80)
- 12 oz. cooked onions
- 4 oz. grated cheese
- 1 teaspoon chopped parsley
- pinch nutmeg
- salt and pepper
- ½ pint white sauce (see page 78)

1 Roll out the pastry thinly and cut into 4-inch rounds.
2 Chop the onions, mix with all other ingredients and season carefully.
3 Put a good spoonful of the mixture on each pastry round. Damp edges and fold over, pressing edges well together.
4 Score across the top of the pastry, put on to a baking tray and bake about 25 minutes in a fairly hot oven (425°F.—Gas Mark 6).

Individual meat pies

cooking time — 20 – 25 minutes

you will need:

- 1 small onion, peeled and chopped finely
- ½ oz. butter
- 8 oz. cooked minced meat
- 1 teaspoon chopped parsley
- pinch mixed herbs
- 2 teaspoons tomato ketchup
- salt and pepper
- stock or gravy
- 6 oz. short crust pastry (see page 80)
- milk

1 Fry onion in butter until lightly browned.
2 Add to the meat together with other flavourings and seasoning.

3 Add enough stock or gravy to make a fairly moist mixture.
4 Roll the pastry thinly and cut into 3½-inch rounds.
5 Line some deep patty tins with half the rounds and fill with meat mixture.
6 Damp edges of the pastry and cover with remaining rounds. Press edges well together and flute with thumb and finger. Make a slit in the top of each pie and brush with milk.
7 Bake for 20 - 25 minutes in a moderately hot oven (400°F.—Gas Mark 5).

Chicken and almond patties

cooking time 20 – 25 minutes

you will need:

1 oz. butter or bacon fat
1 oz. almonds, peeled and shredded
2 rashers bacon
1 medium-sized onion, peeled and finely chopped
1 teaspoon flour
⅛ pint stock
8 oz. cooked minced chicken
salt and pepper
8 oz. short crust pastry (see page 80)
beaten egg or milk

1 Heat the butter or bacon fat, add the almonds and brown lightly, then remove from the pan.
2 Chop the bacon, put into the pan with the onion and fry until onion is soft and lightly coloured.
3 Add the flour and mix well, add stock and stir until boiling, then cook gently for 3 minutes.
4 Stir in the chicken and season mixture carefully. Add almonds.
5 Roll out the pastry and cut into 3½-inch rounds. Line some fairly deep patty pans with half the rounds.
6 Fill with chicken mixture.
7 Damp the edges of pastry and put another round on top, pressing edges well together.
8 Brush with a little egg or milk and bake for 20 - 25 minutes in a fairly hot oven (425°F.—Gas Mark 6).

Ham sausage and egg pie

cooking time 30 – 35 minutes

you will need:

8 oz. short crust pastry (see page 80)
6 oz. cooked ham, minced
4 oz. streaky bacon
freshly ground black pepper
salt
4 eggs
milk or beaten egg for glazing

1 Line a shallow 8-inch pie plate with half the pastry.
2 Add the ham and cover with the sliced frankfurters.
3 Chop the bacon, fry lightly, then sprinkle over frankfurters. Season lightly with salt and pepper.
4 Break eggs on top, then cover with remaining pastry.
5 Flute edges, pressing well together and decorate with leaves made from pastry trimmings.
6 Brush with milk or egg and bake about 30 minutes in a moderate oven (375°F.—Gas Mark 4).

Lobster patties

cooking time 20 minutes

you will need:

8 oz. flaky pastry (see page 81)
1 medium-sized can lobster
¼ pint thick white sauce (see page 78)
1 tablespoon cream
squeeze lemon juice
salt and pepper
pinch paprika
1 teaspoon chopped parsley
beaten egg

1 Roll pastry thinly and cut into 3-inch rounds. Line some fairly deep patty tins with half the rounds.
2 Chop the lobster into small pieces, and add to the sauce with the cream, lemon juice, seasonings and parsley.
3 Put a spoonful into each patty case, moisten the edge of the pastry and put another round on top, pressing the edges well together.
4 Decorate edges as liked, make a hole in the top of each patty with a skewer and brush over with a little beaten egg.
5 Bake about 20 minutes in a hot oven (450°F.—Gas Mark 7).

Pilchard patties

cooking time 25 minutes

you will need:

1 can pilchards
2 oz. grated cheese
1 teaspoon lemon juice
little freshly ground pepper
salt
4 oz. short crust pastry (see page 80)
beaten egg or milk

1. Drain the pilchards and mash well. Add cheese, lemon juice, pepper and a little salt.
2. If necessary add a little of the sauce from the can as the mixture should be fairly moist.
3. Roll out the pastry thinly and cut into 6 - 8 rounds.
4. Put some of the fish mixture in the centre of each, damp edges, fold pastry over and press edges well together.
5. Put on to a baking tray, brush with egg or milk and bake in a hot oven for about 25 minutes (450°F.—Gas Mark 7).

Variation

Substitute shrimps or prawns for pilchards.

Haddock tricornes

cooking time 15 – 20 minutes

you will need:

6 oz. cooked smoked haddock
2 oz. butter
2 oz. grated cheese
cayenne pepper
1 tablespoon milk
1 egg
8 oz. cheese pastry (see page 81)
paprika

1. Flake the fish finely, and add the butter, cheese, cayenne pepper and milk.
2. Beat the egg and add to the mixture, reserving sufficient for glazing.
3. Roll the pastry thinly and cut into 3½-inch rounds.
4. Put a spoonful of the mixture on each round, damp edges and draw them up to the centre, forming a tricorne.
5. Put on to a baking tray, brush with the remaining egg and sprinkle lightly with paprika.
6. Bake about 10 - 15 minutes in a hot oven (450°F.—Gas Mark 7).

Haddock triangles

cooking time 10 – 15 minutes

you will need for 12 savouries:

6 oz. cheese pastry (see page 81)
8 oz. cooked smoked haddock, flaked and boned
½ pint thick cheese sauce (see page 78)
beaten egg or milk for glazing

1. Roll out pastry thinly. Cut into 3½ - 4-inch rounds.
2. Mix the flaked and boned haddock with sauce and place a spoonful in the centre of each round.
3. Brush the outside edges with a little water, draw up over the filling and pinch together to form a three-cornered shape.
4. Brush with a little egg or milk and bake in a hot oven (400°F.—Gas Mark 6) until golden.

Bacon and egg tart

cooking time 40 minutes

you will need:

6 oz. short crust pastry (see page 80)
4 - 6 rashers bacon
3 eggs
salt and pepper
1 tablespoon chopped parsley
4 mushrooms, chopped

1. Line a 7-inch sandwich tin with rather more than half the pastry. Roll out the rest for the pie lid.
2. Arrange the bacon in the pastry case.
3. Beat the eggs, add seasoning, parsley and mushrooms and pour over the bacon.
4. Damp pastry edges, put on lid and press edges well together. Flute with thumb and finger.
5. Bake for 10 minutes in a fairly hot oven (425°F.—Gas Mark 6), then reduce to 350°F. —Gas Mark 3, and cook for a further 30 minutes.

Leek and ham pie

cooking time 1 hour 15 minutes

you will need:

Pastry:
8 oz. flour
pinch salt
5 oz. softened butter

Filling:
4 oz. cooked ham
1 packet leek soup
½ pint milk
¼ pint thin cream
2 eggs
1 oz. cheese, grated

To make the pastry:

1 Sieve flour and salt into a basin.
2 Rub in butter thoroughly, using fingertips.
3 Knead mixture lightly together to form a ball. Chill for 30 minutes.
4 Place dough on a 9-inch pie plate, press out with the fingertips until the plate is completely lined.
5 Prick the sides and bottom well with a fork.
6 Bake blind in a hot oven (425°F.—Gas Mark 7) for 10 - 15 minutes.

To make the filling:

1 Chop the ham roughly and place into the pastry case.
2 Blend the dry leek soup with milk.
3 Stir in the cream and the lightly beaten eggs with a fork.
4 Pour soup mixture into the pastry case.
5 Sprinkle cheese on top.
6 Bake in a slow oven (335°F.—Gas Mark 3) for about 1 hour. Leave until cold.

If the whole pie is to be packed, do not remove from plate.

Asparagus and ham pie

Make as above using 1 packet asparagus instead of leek soup.

Celery and ham pie

Make as above using 1 packet celery instead of leek soup.

American chicken pie

cooking time 30 – 35 minutes

you will need:

8 oz. short crust pastry (see page 80)
4 oz. lean streaky bacon
1 small can pineapple
8 oz. cold cooked chicken
4 oz. cooked green peas
1 tablespoon cream
½ pint white sauce (see page 78)
salt and pepper
beaten egg or milk

1 Line an 8-inch pie plate with rather more than half the pastry.
2 Chop the bacon and fry until the fat begins to run, then add the pineapple cut into small pieces and cook for a few minutes.
3 Chop up the chicken, add the bacon, pineapple and peas.
4 Add the cream to the white sauce, then stir in all other ingredients. Season carefully and pour into pie plate.
5 Damp pastry edges, and cover pie with remaining pastry.
6 Press edges well together and neaten.
7 Brush with egg or milk and make a hole in the top to allow steam to escape.
8 Bake in a fairly hot oven about 30 minutes 425°F.—Gas Mark 6).

Russian fish pasty

cooking time 25 – 30 minutes

you will need:

8 oz. short crust pastry (see page 80)
8 oz. cooked fish
1 oz. butter
1 level tablespoon flour
¼ pint milk
2 - 3 tablespoons canned shrimps (optional)
1 teaspoon chopped parsley
salt
freshly ground black pepper
1 - 2 tablespoons diced cooked beetroot
lemon juice or vinegar
beaten egg or milk

1 Roll the pastry thinly into a large square.
2 Flake the fish, removing any skin and bones.
3 Melt the butter in a pan, add the flour and mix well.
4 Add the milk and any liquor from the shrimps, if used; stir till boiling and boil for 3 minutes.
5 Add parsley, seasoning, fish, beetroot and if necessary a little lemon juice or vinegar. Be sure the mixture is well flavoured and seasoned and leave to cool.
6 Put the square of pastry on to a baking sheet and arrange mixture in the centre. Damp the four corners of the pastry and draw up to the centre.
7 Seal the edges at the centre, but leave a small gap at the side to allow the steam to escape.
8 Brush with egg or milk and bake about 25 minutes in a fairly hot oven (425°F.—Gas Mark 6).

Salmon pie

cooking time 35 – 40 minutes

you will need:

- 8 oz. flaky pastry (see page 81)
- 1 8 oz. can salmon
- 1 tablespoon chopped parsley
- 1 tablespoon lemon juice
- salt
- pinch cayenne pepper
- 1 1 oz. can condensed mushroom soup
- beaten egg or milk to glaze

1 Line an 8-inch pie plate with rather more than half the pastry rolled thinly.
2 Flake the fish finely, removing any black skin and bones. Add parsley, lemon juice, salt and the cayenne pepper.
3 Add the mushroom soup and mix all well.
4 Pour into the pastry case, damp the edges of the pastry and cover with the remaining pastry.
5 Press edges together and knock up with the back of a knife.
6 Brush with egg or milk, score the top and bake for 10 minutes in a hot oven (450°F.—Gas Mark 7), and cook a further 25 - 30 minutes.

Egg and ham pasties

cooking time 20 – 30 minutes

you will need:

- 3 hard-boiled eggs
- 6 oz. cooked ham, minced
- salt and pepper
- made mustard
- 3 - 4 tablespoons white sauce (see page 78)
- 8 oz. short crust pastry (see page 80)
- beaten egg or milk

1 Chop eggs finely.
2 Add the ham and seasonings and bind with the white sauce.
3 Roll the pastry thinly and cut into rounds about 4 inches across.
4 Put a good spoonful of the meat mixture on each pastry round, damp the edges and fold over, pressing edges well together, then flute with the thumb and finger.
5 Put on to a baking tray, brush with egg or milk and bake for about 25 minutes in a fairly hot oven (425°F.—Gas Mark 6).

Ham and egg pie

cooking time 20 minutes

you will need:

- 8 oz. short crust pastry (see page 80)
- 8 oz. finely chopped lean cooked ham
- 6 eggs, lightly beaten
- little onion juice or minced onion
- made mustard
- salt and pepper
- beaten egg or milk

1 Line a pie plate with half the pastry.
2 Mix the ham and eggs together, and season carefully with the onion juice, mustard, salt and pepper.
3 Pour into pastry case, damp edges and cover with remaining pastry, pressing edges well together.
4 Brush with a little egg or milk and bake for 10 minutes in a hot oven (400°F.—Gas Mark 5), and continue cooking for a further 10 minutes.

Egg and mushroom pasty

cooking time 40 – 45 minutes

you will need:

- 4 - 5 hard-boiled eggs
- 1 can condensed mushroom soup
- 3 tablespoons mashed potato
- 2 teaspoons chopped parsley
- salt and pepper
- 8 oz. short crust pastry (see page 80)
- milk

1 Chop the eggs.
2 Put into a pan with soup, potato and parsley.
3 Stir over a low heat until the mixture is hot and well mixed. Season carefully and leave to cool.
4 Roll the pastry into a 9-inch round.
5 Put the egg mixture on one half, damp pastry edges and fold over, pressing edges well together. Flute with thumb and finger.
6 Move carefully on to a baking tray, brush with milk and bake about 40 minutes in a moderately hot oven (400°F.—Gas Mark 5).

Cornish pasties

cooking time about 1 hour

you will need:

- 6 oz. short crust pastry (see page 80)
- salt and pepper
- 4 oz. raw minced meat
- 2 large raw potatoes
- pinch mixed herbs, or 1 teaspoon chopped parsley
- beaten egg or milk

1 Divide the pastry into 4 portions, and roll each into a ¼-inch thick round.
2 Add salt and pepper to the meat and divide equally between pastry rounds.
3 Cover each with the coarsely grated potato and sprinkle with herbs or parsley.
4 Damp pastry edges and draw up so that the edges meet in the centre. Press well together and flute with the thumb and finger.
5 Put on to a baking tray and brush with egg or milk.
6 Bake for 10 minutes in a fairly hot oven (425°F.—Gas Mark 6). Then reduce to 350°F.—Gas Mark 3 and cook for a further 45 - 50 minutes.

Corned beef and egg pie

cooking time 40 – 45 minutes

you will need:

8 oz. short crust pastry (see page 80)
1 can corned beef
1 teaspoon chopped parsley
¼ pint beef stock (a stock cube can be used if no stock is available)
4 eggs
salt and pepper

1 Line a 7 - 7½ inch pie plate with rather more than half the pastry.
2 Mash corned beef well with a fork. Add parsley and enough stock to moisten. The meat mixture should be fairly soft.
3 Put half the mixture into the pastry case. Make four hollows in the meat and into each break 1 egg. Season with salt and pepper.
4 Cover carefully with the rest of the meat.
5 Roll out the remaining pastry for the lid and cover the pie. Press the edges together and decorate as liked.
6 Bake about 40 minutes in a moderately hot oven (450°F.—Gas Mark 5).

Variation

Follow the recipe as above, but add 1 teaspoon tomato purée and ¼ teaspoon oregano to the mashed corned beef. Continue as above.

Cheese flan

cooking time about 20 minutes

you will need:

1 - 2 cooked carrots, sliced
1 tablespoon cooked peas
2 tomatoes, peeled and sliced
1 7-inch baked flan case (see page 80)
2 hard-boiled eggs, sliced
½ pint cheese sauce (see page 78)
½ oz. grated cheese
1 tablespoon breadcrumbs

1 Arrange the vegetables in the flan case in alternate layers with the eggs and sauce, finishing with a layer of sauce.
2 Mix cheese and breadcrumbs together and sprinkle over.
3 Bake about 20 minutes in a moderately hot oven (375°F.—Gas Mark 4).

Cheese and tomato pie

cooking time about 45 minutes

you will need:

8 oz. short crust pastry (see page 80)
2 Spanish onions, peeled and sliced
4 large tomatoes, peeled and sliced
3 oz. grated cheese
salt and pepper
beaten egg or milk

1 Line an 8-inch pie plate with rather more than half the pastry, roll out the rest for the lid.
2 Cook onions in boiling salted water till tender, drain well.
3 Fill pastry case with layers of onion rings, tomato slices and cheese, seasoning lightly between the layers.
4 Damp pastry edges and cover with the lid, pressing edges well together. Flute with thumb and finger.
5 Brush over with egg or milk and bake about 40 minutes in a moderately hot oven (400°F.—Gas Mark 5).

Main Course for a Packed Meal

Packed meals fall into two categories — the lunch box that is carried five days out of seven and the meal that is packed for a day's outing by car, on the scooter or on foot. However, the latter should be considered as a lunch box since it is a meal that is transported personally and therefore the amount of its contents must be somewhat restricted.

How to pack a lunch box

Be sure that the box is scrupulously clean. Line it with clean paper or foil. Put heaviest foods to the bottom, wrapping cold fried chicken, slices of meat loaf, hard-boiled eggs, etc. in foil or greaseproof paper. Pack moist foods in covered plastic containers, if possible, and do not forget one or two tissues or paper napkins for sticky fingers.

To pack a portable meal

While there are magnificent and expensive fitted picnic baskets to be bought, a home-made one can be fun to use and can be built up according to the needs of the family. A large square shopping basket is ideal and it is worth keeping it for this purpose, with all its accessories packed away inside to avoid a last minute scramble, which always results in some vital item being forgotten.

In most cases a vacuum flask is a 'must' for a hot drink, and if yours is the sort of family that frequently enjoys taking a meal out of doors, it is worth investing in an insulated container for keeping food hot or cold.

Other 'musts' include paper napkins or towels, plates, cups or glasses, cutlery and a can and bottle opener, containers for salt, pepper and sugar, a good supply of foil and polythene bags and a face flannel and hand towel, and a box of matches.

Most of these main course dishes can be prepared to provide a made-up meal for mother and any other members of the family who eat at home, so that the one course may be shared and it is not necessary to prepare an additional meal.

Sausage rolls

cooking time 25 - 30 minutes

you will need:

4 oz. short crust pastry (see page 80)
8 oz. sausage meat
beaten egg or milk

1 Roll the pastry into an oblong about 8 inches x 6 inches and cut in half lengthwise.
2 Divide the sausage meat in half and, using floured hands, roll each piece into a long sausage about 8 inches in length.
3 Put 1 piece on to each strip of pastry, damp the edges and roll the pastry over the meat. Be sure the two edges adhere together; leave with the join on the underside.
4 Cut into lengths with a sharp knife and put on to a baking tray. Brush with egg or milk.
5 Bake for 10 minutes in a fairly hot oven (425°F.—Gas Mark 6), then reduce the heat to 350°—Gas Mark 3, and continue cooking a further 15 - 20 minutes.

Sausage and cheese rolls

cooking time 20 - 25 minutes

you will need:

1 lb. sausages
small fingers of cheese
6 oz. flaky pastry (see page 81)
beaten egg or milk

1 Split the sausages lengthwise, insert a finger of cheese and re-form the sausage.
2 Roll the pastry thinly and cut into 8 squares.
3 Put a sausage on each piece of pastry, damp the edges and fold over.
4 Press the edges well together and knock up with the back of a knife.
5 Put on to a baking tray, brush with egg or milk and bake for 20 - 25 minutes in a hot oven (450°F.—Gas Mark 7).

Potato eggs

cooking time 5 – 7 minutes

you will need:

12 oz. boiled potatoes
salt
cayenne pepper
3 oz. grated cheese
2 eggs, beaten
4 hard-boiled eggs
flour for coating
breadcrumbs
deep fat or oil for frying

1 Mash the potatoes and season with salt and cayenne pepper. Add the cheese and sufficient beaten egg to form a fairly stiff smooth paste.
2 Shell hard-boiled eggs and coat lightly with flour.
3 Divide the potato mixture into 4, flatten out each portion on a floured board and mould around the eggs, keeping the original shape.
4 Coat with the remaining beaten egg, roll in breadcrumbs and fry in deep fat till golden brown.

Note

If you prefer oil to fat for frying, heat the oil to 375°F.

Remember that corn oil does not smoke at this temperature, so to check that it is ready for using, drop a 1-inch cube of stale bread into the pan. If the bread drops to the bottom and stays there, the oil is not hot enough. If it rises to the surface immediately and becomes golden brown, the oil is ready.

Kromeskies

cooking time 7 – 10 minutes

you will need:

2 oz. butter
1 small onion, peeled and chopped
2 oz. mushrooms, chopped
1 oz. flour
½ pint meat stock
8 oz. cooked minced meat
pinch mixed herbs
seasoning
8 thin slices cooked ham
fat for frying

Batter for coating:
2 oz. flour
1 egg
¼ pint milk

1 Heat the butter in a pan, add the onion and mushrooms and cook until the onion is soft.
2 Add flour and mix well.
3 Add stock gradually, stirring all the time, until sauce boils and thickens.
4 Add minced meat, herbs and seasoning and leave to get cold.
5 Flour the hands and form the mixture into 8 small sausage shapes.
6 Wrap a slice of ham round each.
7 To make the batter mix the flour to a smooth consistency with the egg and milk.
8 Fry till crisp and golden in deep fat.

Sausage cutlets

cooking time 7 – 10 minutes

you will need:

4 cooked lamb cutlets
8 oz. sausage meat
grated rind 1 lemon
1 level teaspoon finely chopped mint
beaten egg and breadcrumbs for coating
fat for frying

1 Trim the cutlets.
2 Put the sausage meat into a basin, add the lemon rind and mint and mix all well.
3 Divide into 4 and cover each cutlet with sausage meat, pressing it on well and keeping the shape intact.
4 Coat with egg and breadcrumbs and fry in deep fat.

Nut cutlets

cooking time about 10 minutes

you will need:

1 oz. butter
1 oz. flour
½ pint milk
2 teaspoons finely grated onion
4 oz. minced mixed nuts
2 oz. breadcrumbs
½ teaspoon finely chopped parsley
¼ teaspoon ground mace
1 teaspoon lemon juice
salt
about ½ egg
beaten egg and breadcrumbs for coating
deep fat for frying

1 Heat the butter, add the flour and mix well.
2 Add the milk and stir till boiling.
3 Add the onion and cook for a few minutes. Remove from the heat.
4 Add the nuts, breadcrumbs and flavourings and enough egg to bind all well together.
5 Turn on to a wetted plate, smooth the surface and mark into 8 portions. Leave to cool.
6 Form each portion into a cutlet shape, coat with egg and breadcrumbs and fry in deep fat.

Crunchy baked chicken

cooking time 40 – 45 minutes

you will need:

1 chicken quarter
salt
1 rounded tablespoon cornflour
1 small packet potato crisps
little evaporated or top of milk

1. Rub chicken quarter all over with salt then coat evenly with cornflour.
2. Crush potato crisps with a rolling pin on a sheet of greaseproof paper.
3. Dip chicken in milk, drain, then coat thickly and evenly with potato crisp crumbs.
4. Place skin side up on a baking sheet and cook in a moderate oven (350°F.—Gas Mark 4) until tender.
5. Leave on kitchen paper until cold.

Picnic chicken

cooking time about 40 minutes

you will need:

1 tender chicken
1 - 2 tablespoons flour
salt and pepper
1 egg
juice and rind 1 lemon
breadcrumbs
oil

1. Cut the chicken into small joints and coat lightly with flour to which a little salt and pepper has been added.
2. Beat the egg and add the lemon juice.
3. Mix the grated lemon rind with the breadcrumbs.
4. Coat the joints with egg, then breadcrumbs.
5. Heat some oil in a baking tin, put joints in and baste.
6. Cook for about 40 minutes in a moderately hot oven (400°F.—Gas Mark 5).
7. Leave on kitchen paper until cold.

Chicken and ham croquettes

cooking time about 7 – 10 minutes

you will need:

1 oz. butter
1 oz. flour
½ pint milk or chicken stock
6 oz. cooked chopped chicken
2 oz. cooked chopped ham
pinch mixed herbs
salt and pepper
beaten egg
breadcrumbs
fat for frying

1. Melt the butter, add the flour and mix well.
2. Add the milk or stock, stir till boiling and boil for 3 minutes.
3. Remove from the heat, add the chicken, ham, herbs and seasoning. Mix all well together.
4. Turn out on to a wetted plate, smooth the surface and mark into 6 portions. Leave to cool.
5. Shape each portion into a croquette, dip into egg, then breadcrumbs, and fry in deep fat.

Oven fried chicken

cooking time 15 – 20 minutes depending on size of joints

you will need:

3 - 4 tablespoons corn oil
4 chicken joints
1 tablespoon seasoned flour
1 egg
4 tablespoons browned breadcrumbs

1. Pour enough oil in roasting tin or shallow ovenproof dish to cover the bottom.
2. Put the dish into the oven at 375°F.—Gas Mark 5 for 10 minutes to preheat oil.
3. Dip chicken joints in seasoned flour, then in beaten egg and breadcrumbs.
4. Place joints in hot oil, baste well.
5. Bake uncovered until tender.
6. Place on kitchen paper and leave until cold.

Chicken soufflés

you will need:

¼ oz. gelatine
¼ pint aspic jelly
¼ pint white sauce (see page 78)
8 oz. cooked chicken, minced
seasoning
1 small can evaporated milk
2 egg whites

1. Dissolve the gelatine in the liquid aspic jelly (made according to packet instructions) and stir carefully into the white sauce.
2. Add the chicken and seasoning.
3. Whip the evaporated milk until stiff and fold into chicken mixture when it has begun to thicken.
4. Fold in the stiffly beaten egg whites.
5. Spoon quickly into waxed containers.

Chicken puffs

cooking time 15 minutes

you will need:

- 8 oz. flaky or rough pastry (see page 81)
- 8 oz. cooked minced chicken
- 1 - 2 tablespoons cooked green peas
- 2 tablespoons chopped canned pineapple (optional)
- salt and pepper
- 2 - 3 tablespoons white sauce (see page 78)
- beaten egg or milk to glaze

1 Roll the pastry thinly and cut in to 3 - 3½-inch rounds with a plain cutter.
2 Mix the chicken, peas and pineapple together, add seasoning and enough white sauce to bind.
3 Put a spoonful on each round of pastry, damp edges and draw up to the centre, pressing edges well together. Neaten joins and put on to a baking sheet.
4 Brush with a little egg or milk and bake for about 15 minutes in a hot oven (450°F.—Gas Mark 7).

Devilled chicken

cooking time about 10 minutes

you will need:

- 2 tablespoons oil
- ¼ level teaspoon curry powder
- 2 level teaspoons made mustard
- ¼ level teaspoon freshly ground black pepper
- pinch cayenne pepper
- 2 teaspoons vinegar
- 2 teaspoons tomato ketchup
- Joints cold cooked chicken (legs and thighs are most suitable)

1 Mix the oil and curry powder smoothly, then add all other ingredients.
2 Brush generously over the chicken joints and grill on both sides until well browned.

Baconburgers

cooking time 7 – 10 minutes

you will need:

- 8 oz. ham, minced
- 4 oz. sausage meat
- 1 small onion, peeled and minced
- seasoning
- pinch mixed herbs
- 1 egg yolk
- flour
- 2 oz. thinly sliced cheese
- beaten egg and breadcrumbs
- deep fat for frying

1 Mix together ham, sausage meat, onion, seasoning and herbs and bind with egg yolk.
2 Divide into 8 portions.
3 Divide each portion in half and flatten into 2 rounds, using floured hands.
4 Sandwich the 2 rounds together with 1 thin slice of cheese in the middle.
5 Mould into a neat shape, coat with egg and breadcrumbs and fry in deep fat. Allow at least 7 minutes for the sausage meat to be well cooked.

Bacon puffs

cooking time 15 – 20 minutes

you will need:

- 6 oz. flaky pastry (see page 81)
- ½ oz. butter
- ½ oz. flour
- 4 - 6 tablespoons milk
- 4 oz. streaky bacon, minced
- pepper
- grated nutmeg

1 Roll out the pastry and divide into 8 squares.
2 Melt the butter, add the flour and mix well. Add milk gradually, stirring all the time, until mixture boils and thickens. Cook for 1 minute.
3 Add bacon, pepper and nutmeg.
4 Put a spoonful of this mixture on each pastry square, damp edges and fold over to form a triangle. Press edges well together and knock up with the back of a knife.
5 Put on to a baking tray and bake for 15 - 20 minutes in a hot oven till golden brown 450°F.—Gas Mark 7).

Corned beef burgers

cooking time 8 – 10 minutes

you will need:

- 1 12 oz. can corned beef
- 2 oz. fresh white breadcrumbs
- 1 teaspoon mixed herbs
- 1 teaspoon minced onion
- salt and pepper
- 1 egg, beaten
- fat for frying

1 Chop and mash the corned beef finely.
2 Add breadcrumbs, herbs, onion and seasoning and bind to a stiff mixture with the egg.
3 Divide into 4 or 6 portions and shape into flat round cakes with floured hands.
4 Heat some fat and fry cakes till well browned, allowing 4 - 5 minutes for each side.

Celery and egg croquettes

cooking time about 45 minutes

you will need:

1 head celery
milk
1 oz. butter
1 oz. flour
4 hard-boiled eggs
salt and pepper
pinch nutmeg
1 beaten egg yolk
beaten egg and breadcrumbs for coating
deep fat for frying

1 Wash and cut up the celery and stew in a little milk till tender. Then rub through a sieve. This should produce about ½ pint purée.
2 Melt the butter, add the flour and mix well.
3 Add the purée, stir till boiling and boil for 3 minutes.
4 Add the chopped hard-boiled eggs and season carefully, then add the beaten egg yolk and mix well.
5 Turn on to a wetted plate, smooth the top and mark into 6 portions. Leave to cool.
6 Shape into croquettes, coat with egg and breadcrumbs, fry in deep fat.

Danish turnovers

cooking time 20 – 25 minutes

you will need:

2 tablespoons oil
1 onion, peeled and chopped finely
12 oz. raw beef, minced
½ level teaspoon paprika
½ level teaspoon dry mustard
1 tablespoon Worcestershire sauce
pinch garlic salt
pinch celery salt
1 tablespoon sour cream
3 - 4 oz. Danish blue cheese
8 oz. short crust pastry (see page 80)
beaten egg or milk

1 Heat the oil, add the onion and cook till lightly coloured.
2 Add the minced meat and cook gently, stirring frequently with a fork.
3 When the meat is cooked, add paprika, mustard, sauce and salts and allow to cool a little before adding the cream and cheese.
4 Season carefully.
5 Roll pastry thinly and cut into 8 rounds.
6 Put a spoonful of mixture on each round, damp edges and fold over, pressing the edges well together. Flute with thumb and finger and make a slit in the top of the pastry to allow steam to escape.
7 Put on to a baking tray, brush with egg or milk and bake about 25 minutes in a fairly hot oven (425°F. - Gas Mark 6).

Cutlets au gratin

cooking time 25 minutes

you will need:

6 - 8 small lamb cutlets
stock
3 oz. grated cheese
pinch cayenne pepper
1½ oz. dry breadcrumbs
1 egg, beaten
fat for frying

1 Trim the cutlets and simmer for about 15 minutes in a little stock. Remove from the pan and dry in a cloth.
2 Mix the cheese, cayenne pepper and breadcrumbs.
3 Brush the cutlets with the egg, then coat well with the breadcrumb mixture.
4 Fry in shallow fat till crisp and brown on both sides.
5 Drain and leave to get quite cold before packing.

Egg and cheese cutlets

cooking time 7 minutes

you will need:

1 oz. butter
1 oz. flour
½ pint milk
1 oz. grated cheese
pinch cayenne pepper
salt
2 hard-boiled eggs, chopped finely
beaten egg, and breadcrumbs for coating
deep fat for frying

1 Melt the butter, add the flour and mix well.
2 Add the milk, stir till boiling and boil for 3 minutes.
3 Add the cheese, cayenne pepper, salt and eggs; mix all well together.
4 Turn out on to a wetted plate, smooth the surface and divide into 4 portions. Leave to cool.
5 Form each portion into a cutlet shape, coat with egg and breadcrumbs and fry in deep fat.

Ham and egg cake

cooking time about 7 – 10 minutes

you will need:

2 hard-boiled eggs	salt and pepper
4 oz. minced cooked ham	1 teaspoon finely chopped parsley
2 oz. breadcrumbs	beaten egg
2 tablespoons flour	fat for frying

1. Chop eggs very finely and mix with ham, breadcrumbs and flour.
2. Add seasoning and parsley and bind with beaten egg.
3. Shape into flat round cakes and fry till golden brown on both sides.

Fish cakes

cooking time 5 – 7 minutes

you will need:

1 oz. butter	1 teaspoon chopped parsley
1 oz. flour	1 teaspoon lemon juice
½ pint milk	1 teaspoon chopped capers
8 oz. cooked smoked haddock, or 4 oz. smoked haddock and 4 oz. cooked white fish	salt beaten egg and breadcrumbs deep fat for frying

1. Melt the butter, add the flour and mix well.
2. Add the milk, stir till boiling and boil for 3 minutes.
3. Flake the fish finely, removing all skin and bones, and stir into the panada.
4. Add flavourings and seasonings.
5. Turn on to a wetted plate, smooth surface and mark into 6 portions. Leave to cool.
6. Form each portion into a round flat cake, coat with egg and breadcrumbs and fry in deep fat.

Haddock cakes

cooking time 7 – 10 minutes

you will need:

8 oz. cooked smoked haddock	2 teaspoons finely chopped parsley
1 tablespoon grated onion	lemon juice
6 oz. cooked mashed potato	salt 3 - 4 tablespoons thick white sauce (see page 78)
freshly ground black pepper	flour
pinch crushed thyme	fat for frying

1. Flake the fish finely and mix with all other ingredients, except flour, adding enough white sauce to bind.
2. Check the seasoning, adding more lemon juice and salt as required.
3. Spread out on a wetted plate, mark into 6 portions and leave to get cold.
4. Shape into round flat cakes using floured hands.
5. Sprinkle with flour and fry in shallow fat until brown on both sides.

Salmon ring

cooking time 15 – 20 minutes

you will need:

For scone mixture:	
7 oz. plain flour	2 level teaspoons baking powder
1 oz. cornflour	1 oz. butter
pinch salt	milk
For the filling:	
½ oz. butter	2 teaspoons lemon juice
1 level tablespoon cornflour	1 teaspoon chopped capers
½ pint milk	seasoning
1 8 oz. can salmon	milk or beaten egg

To make the scone mixture:

1. Sieve the flour, cornflour, salt and baking powder together.
2. Rub in the butter, and add enough milk to make a pliable dough.
3. Roll thinly into an oblong.

To make the filling:

1. Melt the butter, add the cornflour and cook for a few minutes.
2. Add the milk, stir till boiling and boil for 1 minute.
3. Add the fish, flaked finely, lemon juice, capers and seasoning.
4. Spread the fish mixture on to the scone dough, damp edges and roll up as for a Swiss roll.
5. Place carefully on a greased baking tin and form into a horseshoe.
6. Using a sharp knife, make some cuts all round, about two-thirds of the way into the roll.
7. Open out each section a little on to its side, then brush with milk or egg and bake for 15 - 20 minutes in a hot oven (450°F.—Gas Mark 7).

Sweet Course for a Packed Meal

Almost any pudding made with a blancmange or jelly basis can be safely and easily packed, if prepared and put in waxed cartons or small polythene containers which are excellent for this purpose. Do not forget the spoons.

Fruit salad may be packed in wide-necked preserving or storage jars. A mixture of fresh fruit, as available, and canned fruit does make a refreshing end to the meal.

Individual pies are always popular too and small foil dishes are ideal, for they can be used for cooking and transportation. Do make sure that the filling is not too runny.

If you find that these items make packing a problem, a slice of home-made cake or a few biscuits will usually satisfy the sweet-toothed, and of course some fresh fruit is always appreciated. A fruit cake of the cut-and-come-again variety, gingerbread or freshly baked sandwich cake are good travellers, but avoid sticky fillings or icing.

Devonshire pielets

cooking time about 30 minutes

you will need:

- 8 oz. short crust pastry (see page 80)
- 1 large apple, peeled, cored and chopped
- 1 dessertspoon currants
- 2 tablespoons dry breadcrumbs
- 1 large tablespoon marmalade
- grated rind and juice of 1 lemon
- 1 tablespoon brown sugar
- egg white
- castor sugar

1. Roll the pastry thinly and cut into rounds with a 3-inch plain cutter.
2. Line some patty tins with half the rounds.
3. Mix all the ingredients for the filling well together and fill the pastry cases.
4. Damp the edges and cover with another round of pastry, pressing the edges well together.
5. Brush with egg white or water and sprinkle with castor sugar.
6. Bake about 30 minutes in a moderately hot oven (400°F.—Gas Mark 5).

Date crunch

cooking time 45 minutes

you will need:

- 4 oz. dates
- ¼ pint water
- 1½ oz. flour
- 3 oz. butter
- 4 oz. rolled oats
- 1½ oz. sugar

1. Stone and chop the dates and cook in the water till soft, then leave to cool.
2. Mix the flour and oats together and rub in the butter, add the sugar and mix well.
3. Put half this mixture into a greased sandwich tin and press down firmly.
4. Spread the date mixture on top and cover with the rest of the oats mixture.
5. Smooth the top and press well down.
6. Bake for about 45 minutes in a moderate oven (375°F.—Gas Mark 4).
7. Mark into slices and leave in the tin.

Gooseberry tart

cooking time about 40 minutes

you will need:

- 8 oz. flaky pastry (see page 81)
- 1 lb. gooseberries
- ¼ pint water
- 4 oz. sugar
- 2 level teaspoons cornflour

To glaze:

- egg white
- sugar

1. Divide the pastry in half, roll out thinly and line a pie plate with half the pastry, reserving the rest for the lid.
2. Top, tail and wash the gooseberries and put them into a pan with the water. Cook very gently until they are just tender, then drain off the juice.
3. Measure out ¼ pint and put it back into the pan with the sugar.
4. Mix the cornflour smoothly with 1 tablespoon of the remaining juice. Add to the pan, stir till boiling and boil for 1 minute.
5. Put the gooseberries back into this thickened syrup, and when cool, pour into the pie plate.
6. Damp the edges of the pastry and cover with the lid, pressing the edges well together. Cut off any surplus pastry and knock up the edges with the back of a knife, decorating as liked.

7 Brush with egg white and sprinkle with sugar.
8 Cook for 10 minutes in a hot oven (450°F.—Gas Mark 7), then reduce the heat to 400°F.—Gas Mark 5 and cook a further 25 - 30 minutes.

Bakewell tart

cooking time 30 minutes

you will need:

6 - 8 oz. jam	1 egg white
1 baked pastry case (see page 80)	8 oz. sugar
4 egg yolks	8 oz. butter, melted
	1 lemon

1 Spread the jam fairly thickly over the pastry case.
2 Beat the egg yolks, add egg white, sugar and melted butter.
3 Add grated lemon rind and lemon juice and mix all well together.
4 Pour this mixture over the jam.
5 Bake for about 30 minutes in a very moderate oven (325°F.—Gas Mark 2).

Apple cake

cooking time 25 – 30 minutes

you will need:

8 oz. short crust pastry (see page 80)	1 teaspoon grated lemon rind
1 lb. cooking apples	water
3 - 4 oz. sugar	1 egg white

1 Cut the pastry in half and roll into two rounds the size of a meat plate.
2 Put one round on to a greased baking tin.
3 Peel and slice the apples very thinly and arrange on the pastry to within one inch of the edge.
4 Sprinkle with sugar and lemon rind and add 1 tablespoon water. Moisten the edge of the pastry.
5 Cover with the second round, press the edges well together and pinch into flutes with the thumb and finger.
6 Brush over with egg white and sprinkle generously with sugar.
7 Bake about 25 minutes in a fairly hot oven (425°F.—Gas Mark 6).

Apple and cheese slices

cooking time 40 – 45 minutes

you will need:

8 oz. short crust pastry (see page 80)	3 oz. sultanas
1½ lb. cooking apples	2 - 3 oz. sugar
	4 oz. grated cheese

1 Line an 8-inch pie plate or sandwich tin with half the pastry.
2 Peel, core and grate the apples and mix with the sultanas, sugar and cheese.
3 Put into the pastry case, moisten the edge and cover with the remaining pastry.
4 Press the edges well together, make a slit in the top of the pastry and decorate the edges as liked. Mark into 8 portions with the back of a knife.
5 Bake for 20 minutes in a fairly hot oven (425°F.—Gas Mark 6), then reduce the heat to 375°F.—Gas Mark 4, and continue the cooking for a further 20 - 25 minutes.

Fairy creams

cooking time about 10 minutes

you will need:

1 pint water	3 level tablespoons cornflour
rind and juice of 1 large lemon	few drops cochineal
3 tablespoons sugar	2 egg whites

1 Put the water into a pan with the thinly pared lemon rind, lemon juice and sugar.
2 Heat very slowly to boiling point and boil for 3 minutes.
3 Mix the cornflour smoothly with a little cold water.
4 When the syrup has cooled a little, strain on to the mixed cornflour, stirring well.
5 Return to the pan, stir till boiling and boil for 3 minutes, stirring all the time.
6 Add a few drops of cochineal to give a delicate pink colour.
7 Beat the egg whites stiffly and fold into the mixture.
8 Put into waxed containers or wetted dariole moulds and leave to set.

Apple creams

cooking time 10 – 15 minutes

you will need:

2 lbs. cooking apples
juice and grated rind of 1 lemon
½ pint water
4 oz. sugar
2 oz. preserved ginger, chopped
2 tablespoons ginger syrup
½ oz. gelatine
¼ pint thick cream
cochineal (optional)

1 Cook the peeled and cored apples to a pulp with the lemon juice and rind and water.
2 Add the sugar, and rub all through a sieve.
3 Measure the quantity of purée and make it up to 1 pint, if necessary, with water.
4 Add the chopped ginger and the gelatine dissolved in the ginger syrup.
5 When cool, but not set, fold in the half whipped cream.
6 A few drops of colouring may be added to give a pale pink colour.
7 Pour into individual waxed containers.

Apple and date turnovers

cooking time 25 minutes

you will need:

6 oz. biscuit crust (see page 82)
12 oz. cooking apples
2 - 3 oz. sugar
4 oz. dates
pinch of ground cinnamon
little grated lemon rind

1 Roll the pastry thinly and cut into oblong pieces about 4 inches x 8 inches.
2 Peel and core the apples and slice them thinly.
3 Put the apples into a basin with the sugar, dates, stoned and chopped, cinnamon and lemon rind and mix all well together.
4 Put some of this mixture on to each piece of pastry. Damp the edges and fold over to form a square.
5 Press the edges well together and flute with the thumb and finger.
6 Bake for about 25 minutes in a fairly hot oven (425°F.—Gas Mark 6).

Apple and date tart

cooking time 40 minutes

you will need:

8 oz. short crust pastry (see page 80)
1 lb. cooking apples
1 oz. sponge cake crumbs
1 oz. chopped hazel nuts
3 oz. dates, stoned and chopped
2 oz. sugar

To glaze:
egg white
sugar
water

1 Line an 8-inch pie plate with rather more than half the pastry.
2 Peel and core the apples and grate fairly coarsely.
3 Mix the apples with the cake crumbs, nuts, dates and sugar and spread over the pastry.
4 Damp the rim of the pastry and cover with the rest of the dough, pressing the edges well together.
5 Brush with lightly beaten egg white and sprinkle with sugar or brush with a sugar and water syrup glaze.
6 Bake for 15 minutes in a fairly hot oven (425°F.—Gas Mark 6), then reduce to 375°F.—Gas Mark 4 and continue cooking a further 25 minutes.

Fresh fruit salad

you will need:

2 lb. fresh fruit in season
½ pint water
juice of ½ lemon
8 oz. sugar

1 Put the water, lemon juice and sugar together. Heat slowly until the sugar has dissolved, then boil for 5 minutes. Leave to get cold.
2 Prepare the fruit according to its kind and cut into fairly small pieces. A few maraschino cherries can be added to give colour.
3 Pour the syrup over and pack into a screw top jar or container.

Note

Do not add bananas to a fruit salad unless it is to be eaten at once.

Damson fruit jelly

cooking time about 15 minutes

you will need:

1 lb. damsons
4 oz. sugar
water
2½ oz. cornflour

1 Wash the damsons and put into a pan with the sugar and enough water just to cover. Cook gently until the damsons are quite soft, then rub all through a sieve.
2 Measure the quantity of purée and make up to 1½ pints with water.
3 Mix the cornflour smoothly with a little cold water, and stir into the purée.
4 Bring to boiling point, stirring all the time and boil for 3 minutes.
5 Pour into waxed cartons and leave to set.

Fruit in jelly

you will need:

- 1 packet orange jelly
- 1 pint orange juice, canned, or orange squash
- 4 oz. grapes, skinned and seeded
- 1 small apple, peeled and diced
- 1 pear, peeled and diced
- 2 bananas
- 1 orange, peeled and divided into sections
- few almonds (optional)

1 Put the jelly tablet into a pan with the orange juice and heat gently until the tablet has dissolved.
2 Leave in a cool place until the jelly begins to thicken, then stir in the fruit carefully, mixing it in as evenly as possible.
3 Spoon into waxed containers and leave to set.

Banana trifles

you will need:

- 1 Swiss roll
- 3 - 4 tablespoons sherry
- 2 tablespoons apricot jam
- 3 - 4 bananas
- juice of ½ lemon
- 1 oz. sugar
- ½ pint custard (see page 79)

1 Thinly slice Swiss roll and put one into the bottom of individual waxed picnic dishes.
2 Sprinkle each slice with a little sherry and spread with jam.
3 Peel the bananas and mash with lemon juice and sugar. Spread a layer over the jam.
4 Cover with another slice of Swiss roll, top with custard. Press down lightly and leave for a little while to allow the sponge to absorb the custard.
5 When cold, decorate as liked with almonds or glacé cherries.

Note

It is not advisable to use cream for decorating dishes which have to be transported.

Upside-down trifles

cooking time 10 minutes

you will need:

- 1 packet jelly
- 2 slices sponge or plain cake
- 2 tablespoons jam or stewed fruit
- sherry or fruit juice (optional)
- ½ pint thick custard (see page 79)

1 Make up 1 pint jelly according to instructions on the packet, leave in a cool place.
2 Crumble cake into the bottom of 4 individual dishes or containers. Add jam or fruit.
3 Moisten with sherry or fruit juice.
4 Pour a thick layer of custard into each dish. Leave in cold place until set.
5 Spoon the jelly, which should be thick but not quite set, over each.
6 Leave in a cool place until set.

Apple and raspberry cream

cooking time 10 – 15 minutes

you will need:

- 1 lb. cooking apples
- water
- 3 - 4 oz. sugar
- fruit juice
- 1 packet raspberry flavoured cornflour
- 1 6 oz. can evaporated milk
- cochineal (optional)

1 Stew peeled and cored apples in a little water until tender and beginning to pulp.
2 Add sugar to taste, beat until a smooth purée is formed.
3 Make the purée up to ¾ pint, with water or fruit juice, if necessary.
4 Blend cornflour to a smooth cream with 2 tablespoons water.
5 Stir into purée, bring to the boil, allow to boil for 1 minute, stirring all the time.
6 Whisk the milk (chilled if possible) until thick.
7 Fold into purée, adding a few drops of colouring.
8 Pour into a large container or individual dishes and leave to become cold and set.
9 Decorate as liked.

Clementine creams

cooking time 5 minutes

you will need:

1 packet lemon flavoured cornflour	1 can mandarin oranges
1 pint milk	desiccated coconut (optional)
3 - 4 tablespoons sugar	glacé cherries (optional)

1. Blend cornflour to a smooth cream with 2 - 3 tablespoons milk taken from 1 pint.
2. Bring remainder of the milk to the boil, pour on to the mixed cornflour, stirring well.
3. Return to the pan, bring back to the boil, allow to boil for 1 minute, stirring all the time.
4. Stir in sugar to taste. Allow blancmange to cool.
5. Drain mandarin oranges, chop roughly. Divide between 4 individual dishes or cartons.
6. Fill dishes with blancmange. Sprinkle with coconut and leave to set.
7. Decorate with a cherry in the centre of each.

Note

Any combination of stewed or canned fruit and flavoured cornflour may be used to make this sweet.

Jellied peach melba

cooking time 10 minutes

you will need:

1 packet vanilla flavoured cornflour	1 raspberry jelly
1 pint milk	1 medium-sized can peaches
3 - 4 tablespoons sugar	

1. Blend cornflour to a smooth cream with 2 - 3 tablespoons milk taken from 1 pint.
2. Bring remainder of milk to boil, pour on to cornflour, stirring well.
3. Return to the pan, bring back to the boil, for 1 minute, stirring all the time.
4. Stir in sugar to taste. Pour into 4 individual containers or dishes and leave to set.
5. Make up jelly according to instructions on the packet and leave in a cool place.
6. Drain peaches, halves or slices may be used, and arrange on top of set blancmange.
7. Spoon jelly, which should be thick but not set, over the peaches and leave until set.

Pineapple whip

cooking time 10 minutes

you will need:

1 can pineapple	3 - 4 tablespoons sugar
1 packet pineapple flavoured cornflour	1 knob of butter
	1 egg

1. Drain the pineapple, make the juice up to ¾ pint with water.
2. Blend the cornflour and sugar to a thin cream with a little of the juice.
3. Bring the remaining juice to the boil.
4. Pour on to the cornflour, stirring.
5. Return to the pan, bring back to the boil, allow to boil for 1 minute, stirring.
6. Remove from heat, stir in the butter and beaten egg yolk. Cook for a further minute, stirring, but do not allow mixture to boil again.
7. Whisk the egg white until stiff, fold into the mixture.
8. Stir in the pineapple, reserving a few pieces for decoration.
9. Pour into individual dishes or containers.
10. Decorate with remaining pineapple and leave in a cool place to set.

Cakes and biscuits

Everyday cake

cooking time 1¼ - 1½ hours

you will need:

8 oz. self-raising flour	5 oz. sugar
4 oz. margarine	2 eggs
8 oz. dried fruit	5 tablespoons milk

1. Grease and line a 6-inch cake tin or a 2-lb. loaf tin.
2. Sieve the flour.
3. Rub in the margarine, add the fruit and sugar and mix well.
4. Beat the eggs with the milk and stir into the dry ingredients.
5. Turn into the prepared tin and bake for 1¼ - 1½ hours in a moderate oven (350°F.—Gas Mark 4).
6. Cool on a wire tray.

Madeira cake

cooking time 1 – 1¾ hours

you will need:

8 oz. flour
pinch salt
1 teaspoon baking powder
5 oz. butter or margarine
5 oz. sugar
finely grated rind 1 lemon
3 eggs
milk to mix, about 3 tablespoons
citron peel (optional)

1. Grease and line a 6-inch cake tin.
2. Sieve the flour, salt and baking powder.
3. Cream the fat and sugar, and add the lemon rind.
4. Gradually beat in the eggs.
5. Fold in the flour, adding the milk to give a soft dropping consistency.
6. Put into the prepared tin, bake for 1 - 1¾ hours in a moderate oven (350°F.—Gas Mark 4).
7. If citron peel is used, cut into strips and carefully place 2 or 3 strips on the top of the cake after it has been in the oven for about 30 minutes.

One-stage fruit cake

cooking time 2 – 2¼ hours

you will need:

12 oz. self-raising flour
6 oz. luxury margarine
6 oz. sugar
1½ level teaspoons mixed spice
12 oz. mixed dried fruit
3 eggs
4 tablespoons milk

1. Grease and line a round 7-inch cake tin.
2. Place all the ingredients in a large mixing bowl.
3. Beat together for about 1 minute until all the ingredients are well mixed.
4. Place mixture in the prepared tin.
5. Smooth the top.
6. Bake for 2 - 2¼ hours in middle of a very moderate oven (335°F.—Gas Mark 3).
7. Remove and cool on a wire tray.

Queen's tart

cooking time 40 minutes

you will need:

6 oz. short crust or flan pastry (see page 80)
3 oz. margarine
3 oz. sugar
1 egg
3 oz. flour
a little milk
2 - 3 oz. glacé cherries
white glacé icing (see page 85)

1. Line an 8-inch pie plate with pastry and prick lightly.
2. Cream margarine and sugar, and gradually beat in the egg.
3. Fold in the flour, adding enough milk to make a soft consistency.
4. Stir in the cherries and spread mixture on to the pastry case.
5. Bake for 40 minutes at 425°F.—Gas Mark 7.
6. Leave until cold, then spread with white glacé icing flavoured with almond essence or lemon juice. Decorate with halved glacé cherries.

Princess tart

Make as above, adding chopped mixed peel instead of cherries and ice with lemon or orange glacé icing (see page 85).

Victoria sandwich

cooking time 25 minutes

you will need:

4 oz. butter or margarine
4 oz. sugar
2 eggs
4 oz. self-raising flour
water or milk — about 1 tablespoon*
jam
icing sugar

*If large eggs are used, additional liquid is not necessary, but water or milk may be added with the egg to give a soft dropping consistency.
For 8-inch sandwich tins you will need:
3 eggs and 6 oz. fat, sugar and self-raising flour. Bake for 30 - 35 minutes.

1. Grease two 7-inch sandwich tins and dust with flour, or line with paper.
2. Cream the fat and sugar.
3. Beat in the eggs gradually.
4. Fold in the sieved flour.
5. Divide between the tins, making sure the mixture is level.
6. Bake for 25 minutes on the top shelf of a moderately hot oven (375°F.—Gas Mark 5).
7. Turn on to a wire rack to cool. When cold sandwich together with jam, and dust the top liberally with icing sugar.

Raisin cakes

cooking time 15 – 20 minutes

you will need:

- 4 oz. short crust pastry (see page 80)
- 8 oz. seedless raisins
- 6 walnut halves
- about 2 tablespoons lemon juice
- 1 oz. brown sugar

1. Line 10 patty tins with the pastry.
2. Mince the raisins and nuts, or chop very finely.
3. Moisten with lemon juice, add half the sugar.
4. Put a spoonful of the mixture into each pastry case and sprinkle with sugar.
5. Bake for 15 - 20 minutes in a hot oven (400°F.—Gas Mark 6).

Viennese shortcakes

cooking time 20 minutes

you will need:

- 4 oz. self-raising flour
- 4 oz. plain flour
- 7 oz. butter
- 2 oz. icing sugar
- ½ teaspoon vanilla essence
- butter cream (see page 85)

1. Grease two baking sheets.
2. Sieve the flours together.
3. Cream fat and sugar, adding vanilla essence.
4. Beat in the flour, working the mixture with a wooden spoon until smooth.
5. Put mixture into a forcing bag fitted with a large rose nozzle.
6. Pipe mixture in circles or strips on to the trays.
7. Bake for 20 minutes in a moderately hot oven (375°F.—Gas Mark 5).
8. Cool on a wire tray. When cold, sandwich with butter cream.

Sugar biscuits

cooking time 15 – 20 minutes

you will need:

- 6 oz. self-raising flour
- pinch salt
- 1 oz. cornflour
- 4 oz. butter
- 4 oz. sugar
- 1 egg
- vanilla essence
- castor sugar

1. Sieve flour, salt and cornflour.
2. Rub in the butter and add the sugar.
3. Beat the egg with a few drops of essence and stir into the flour.
4. Work to a firm dough. Roll out on a floured surface and cut into fancy shapes.
5. Place on a baking sheet and bake for 15 - 20 minutes at 375°F.—Gas Mark 5.
6. Leave on a wire tray to cool. Dust with castor sugar.

Orange or lemon biscuits

Make as above, adding a little finely-grated orange or lemon rind to the sieved flour. Coat the cold biscuits with orange or lemon glacé icing (see page 85).

Spicy biscuits

Make as above, adding ½ teaspoon mixed spice to the flour before sieving. Coat the cold biscuits with white glacé icing (see page 85) and decorate with slices of preserved ginger.

German biscuits

cooking time 10 – 15 minutes

you will need:

- 4 oz. flour
- 2½ oz. butter
- 1 oz. castor sugar
- redcurrant jelly
- white glacé icing (see page 85)
- glacé cherries

1. Sieve the flour. Rub in the fat and add the sugar.
2. Knead the mixture until it forms a smooth dough.
3. Roll out and cut into rounds with a small cutter or wine glass.
4. Bake for 10 - 15 minutes in a slow oven (335°F.—Gas Mark 3) until lightly coloured.
5. Leave on a wire tray until cold.
6. Spread half the biscuits with redcurrant jelly and cover with the remaining biscuits.
7. Ice the top of the biscuits and decorate each with a glacé cherry.

Coffee German biscuits

Make as previous recipe, icing with coffee glacé icing (see page 85) and decorate with halved walnuts.

Lemon German biscuits

Make as above. Sandwich together with lemon curd, ice with chocolate glacé icing (see page 85) and decorate with halved blanched almonds.

Ginger nuts

cooking time 15 - 20 minutes

you will need:

- 4 oz. self-raising flour
- 2 level teaspoons ground ginger
- 1 level teaspoon ground cinnamon
- 1 level dessertspoon sugar
- ½ teaspoon bicarbonate soda
- 2 oz. white vegetable fat
- 2 tablespoons golden syrup

1. Sieve all the dry ingredients.
2. Melt the fat and syrup over a low heat and allow to cool.
3. Stir into the dry ingredients, mixing well with a wooden spoon.
4. Take pieces, about the size of a walnut and roll into a ball between the palms of the hands.
5. Place well apart on a greased baking tray, flatten slightly.
6. Bake at 375°F.—Gas Mark 5 for 15 - 20 minutes.

Coconut rockies

cooking time 10 - 12 minutes

you will need:

- 5 oz. self-raising flour
- pinch salt
- 4 oz. margarine
- 4 oz. sugar
- 1 egg, small
- 3 oz. desiccated coconut

1. Sieve the flour and salt.
2. Cream fat and sugar, and beat in the egg.
3. Stir in the flour and coconut.
4. Half fill small paper cases with the mixture.
5. Place on a baking sheet and bake in a hot oven 425°F.—Gas Mark 7 for 10 - 12 minutes.
6. Cool on a wire tray.

Basic scone mixture

cooking time small scones 7 – 10 minutes
scone round 10 – 15 minutes

you will need:

- 8 oz. flour
- 2 teaspoons baking powder
- ¼ teaspoon salt
- 2 oz. fat (butter, margarine or lard)
- 1 oz. sugar
- ¼ pint milk
- beaten egg or milk for glazing

1. Grease and flour a baking tray.
2. Sieve flour, baking powder and salt.
3. Rub fat into the flour.
4. Add the sugar and any other ingredients to be used (see following recipes).
5. Stir in the milk and mix quickly to a soft dough.
6. Turn on to a floured surface. Flour hands and form the dough into a ball. Cut in half.
7. Press each half lightly by hand, or roll into ¾ inch rounds.
8. Cut out with a 2-inch cutter or divide each round into quarters with a sharp knife. Do not cut through.
9. Place on the baking tray, brush with beaten egg or milk.
10. Bake for 7 - 10 or 10 - 15 minutes in a hot oven (425°F.—Gas Mark 7).
11. Cool on a wire tray. Serve hot or cold.

Cheese scones

Make the basic recipe, omitting the sugar and adding 4 oz. grated cheese and a pinch of dry mustard.

Fancy scones

Make the basic recipe, adding 1 oz. chopped mixed peel and 1 oz. chopped glacé cherries.

Fruit scones

Make the basic recipe, adding 2 oz. currants, sultanas or raisins.

Tea scones

Add 1 beaten egg to the basic recipe and use a little less milk. Serve hot with butter or cream and strawberry or raspberry jam.

Meat and Fish Loaves and Rolls

Meat loaf

cooking time 1½ hours

you will need:

- 1½ lb. raw minced beef
- 4 rashers bacon, chopped
- 1 tablespoon chopped chives
- 1 tablespoon horseradish cream (see page 78)
- salt
- freshly ground black pepper
- 3 oz. breadcrumbs
- 12 oz. tomatoes, peeled, seeded and chopped

1 Mix all ingredients well together and check that the mixture is well seasoned.

2 Put into a greased loaf tin or cake tin and cover with foil or greased paper.

3 Bake for 1½ hours in a very moderate oven (350°F.—Gas Mark 3).

4 Turn out when cool, or leave in the tin for transportation.

Moray meat loaf

cooking time 2½ hours

you will need:

- 2 hard-boiled eggs
- 1 tomato, peeled and sliced
- 1 lb. stewing beef
- ½ small onion
- 4 oz. bacon
- salt, pepper
- pinch mixed herbs
- 4 oz. white breadcrumbs
- 1 egg, well-beaten
- stock

1 Grease a 2-pint pudding basin or mould, and decorate the bottom with a few slices of egg and tomato.

2 Mince the beef, onion and bacon.

3 Add seasonings, mixed herbs and breadcrumbs and mix all well.

4 Add the well-beaten egg and a little stock if the mixture is not sufficiently moist.

5 Put half into the basin, cover with egg slices, then add the rest of the meat.

6 Cover securely with foil or greaseproof paper and steam for 2½ hours.

Pork roll

cooking time about 2½ hours

you will need:

- 1 lb. pork
- 1 lb. lean ham
- 1 dessertspoon chopped onion
- ½ pint white sauce (see page 78)
- 1 egg, beaten
- salt and pepper
- ¼ level teaspoon powdered sage
- 3 - 4 bacon rashers
- stock or water
- aspic jelly (optional)

1 Mince pork, ham and onion twice.

2 Add the white sauce, egg, seasoning and sage.

3 Mix all well together and shape into a roll.

4 Sprinkle a pudding cloth with flour, arrange bacon rashers on it and put the meat roll on top. Roll up in the cloth and tie ends securely.

5 Boil gently for about 2½ hours in stock or water. If water is used, add 1 tablespoon vinegar and 1 level teaspoon salt.

6 When cooked, remove roll and put between two plates with a weight on top. Leave until cold, then remove cloth and pour over a little aspic jelly (made according to packet directions).

Meat galantine

cooking time 2¾ hours

you will need:

- 12 oz. minced beef, veal or pork
- 2 oz. breadcrumbs
- 1 onion, finely chopped
- 3 oz. shredded suet
- seasoning
- 1 egg, beaten
- good pinch mixed herbs
- 2 - 3 hard-boiled eggs
- extra breadcrumbs

1 Mix the meat, breadcrumbs, onion, suet and seasoning together and bind with egg.

2 Form into a neat roll or press out into an oblong. Place the eggs on this and roll tightly.

3 Dip a cloth in boiling water, flour well and wrap the galantine in this. Steam for 2¾ hours.

4 Unwrap the cloth and roll the galantine, while still warm, in crisp breadcrumbs.

5 Cut into slices when cold, and use as a sandwich filling or pack whole and serve with a crisp, fresh salad.

Potato and ham rolls

cooking time 20 – 25 minutes

you will need:

1 lb. cooked potatoes
4 oz. finely minced ham
1 oz. butter
2 eggs, beaten
salt, pepper
2 teaspoons finely chopped parsley

1. Mash the potatoes while still hot; add the ham and butter.
2. Add enough egg to bind, season with salt and pepper. Add parsley.
3. Shape into rolls, brush with the remaining egg and bake in a moderately hot oven for about 20 minutes, or until nicely browned (400°F.—Gas Mark 5).

Angler's roll

cooking time about 30 minutes

you will need:

8 oz. rough puff or flaky pastry (see page 81)
½ small onion, peeled and chopped
1 oz. butter
4 oz. mushrooms, chopped
1 medium-sized can tuna
1 egg
2 teaspoons lemon juice
1 teaspoon chopped capers
salt and pepper

1. Roll the pastry thinly into an oblong and put on to a baking sheet.
2. Fry the onion in butter until beginning to soften, then add the mushrooms and cook for a few minutes.
3. Add the fish, flaked finely, beaten egg, lemon juice and capers. Season carefully.
4. Put the mixture on to the centre of the pastry, damp edges, and fold over, first the top and bottom and then the sides. Press edges well together.
5. Score once or twice across the top, brush with milk and bake for 15 minutes in a hot oven (450°F.—Gas Mark 7). Then reduce to 400°F.—Gas Mark 5 and cook for a further 15 minutes.

No-cook salmon loaf

you will need:

1 8 oz. can salmon
4 oz. cucumber, chopped finely
8 oz. cooked potatoes, diced
2 hard-boiled eggs, chopped
1 teaspoon chopped parsley
seasoning
mayonnaise (see page 79)

1. Flake the salmon finely, removing any black skin and bones.
2. Add cucumber, potatoes, eggs and parsley.
3. Season carefully and add 1 - 2 tablespoons mayonnaise.
4. Press into a greased loaf tin or plastic container and leave, preferably in the refrigerator, for several hours.

Note

This should be transported in the container and served with lettuce and tomatoes.

Chicken and ham roll

cooking time ¾ – 1 hour

you will need:

8 oz. short crust pastry (see page 80)
1½ oz. butter
1 small onion, peeled and chopped
1 oz. flour
¼ pint chicken stock or milk
12 oz. minced cooked chicken
4 oz. minced cooked ham
salt, pepper
2 oz. breadcrumbs
3 hard-boiled eggs
beaten egg or milk

1. Melt butter, add onion and cook for a few minutes. Add flour, mix well and cook for 3 minutes.
2. Add stock or milk gradually, stir till boiling and boil for 3 minutes.
3. Add chicken, ham, seasonings and breadcrumbs and mix well.
4. Turn on to a floured board and press into an oblong shape. Put eggs in the centre and mould meat mixture around them, forming a roll.
5. Roll pastry into an oblong. Put the meat roll in the centre and wrap pastry around.
6. Cut off any surplus pastry and press edges well together.
7. Move carefully to a baking tin, with pastry seam downwards.
8. Brush with egg or milk and score across top of the roll to allow steam to escape.
9. Bake about 45 minutes in moderately hot oven (400°F.—Gas Mark 5).

Chicken and tongue loaf

cooking time — no cooking

you will need:

- 8 oz. cooked chicken
- 4 oz. tongue
- 4 oz. ham
- 1 small red pepper
- 6 olives
- ½ oz. gelatine
- 1 chicken stock cube
- ½ pint hot water

1. Chop chicken, tongue and ham and mix together.
2. Remove the seeds and chop the peppers finely.
3. Mix with the meat and add the chopped olives.
4. Dissolve the gelatine and stock cube in the water, cool a little, then mix with other ingredients.
5. Pour into a loaf tin and leave to set.

Beef loaf

cooking time — 2 - 2½ hours

you will need:

- 2 lb. lean stewing steak
- 1 small onion, peeled
- 1 teaspoon chopped parsley
- 4 oz. fat bacon, chopped
- 6 oz. breadcrumbs
- salt, pepper
- pinch grated nutmeg
- pinch allspice
- 2 eggs
- stock or water
- meat glaze*

*A quick glaze can be made by dissolving 1 meat stock cube and 1 teaspoon gelatine in 2 tablespoons water. Mix together and heat gently.

1. Remove excess fat and any gristle from the meat and mince with the onion.
2. Add parsley, bacon, breadcrumbs, seasoning and spices.
3. Bind with beaten eggs, adding a little stock if required for additional moisture. Mix very well together.
4. Press into a greased loaf tin, cover with greased paper or foil and bake in a very moderate oven for 2 - 2½ hours (350°F.—Gas Mark 3).
5. When the loaf is cooked, remove from oven, put a weight on top and leave overnight in the tin in a cool place.
6. Turn out, and brush with a little meat glaze.

This meat loaf can be transported easily if wrapped in foil and it will be firm enough to cut easily into slices.

Beef and bacon roll

cooking time — about 2 hours

you will need:

- 1 lb. stewing steak
- 1 lb. lean bacon
- 1 small onion, peeled
- 2 oz. breadcrumbs
- 2 oz. hazel nuts or peanuts, chopped
- 1 tablespoon Worcestershire sauce
- 1 egg
- 1 level teaspoon salt, pepper
- 1 teaspoon chopped parsley
- browned breadcrumbs

1. Finely mince meat, bacon and onion together.
2. Add breadcrumbs, nuts, sauce, beaten egg and seasoning and mix all very well.
3. Shape into a roll and wrap securely in aluminium foil.
4. Put on to a baking tray and cook for about 2 hours in a very slow oven (325°F.—Gas Mark 2).
5. When cooked, cool a little before removing the foil, then roll in breadcrumbs and leave to get quite cold and firm.

Beef and mushroom loaf

cooking time — about 1 hour 5 minutes

you will need:

- 1 small tin loaf
- 1 tablespoon melted butter

For the filling:

- 1 oz. butter
- 1 small onion, peeled and finely chopped
- 1 lb. raw minced beef
- 4 oz. mushrooms, peeled and chopped
- salt, pepper
- paprika
- ¼ pint stock or gravy
- 2 tablespoons breadcrumbs

1. Cut a slice lengthways from the top of the loaf.
2. Remove the crumbs from the inside carefully and use this to make the breadcrumbs.
3. Brush the case inside and out with melted butter, put on to a baking sheet with the lid and bake about ½ hour in a moderate oven (375°F.—Gas Mark 4).
4. Heat the butter, add the onion and cook till soft and lightly browned.
5. Add the meat and mushrooms and cook slowly for a few minutes, stirring well with a fork to break up the meat.
6. Add seasoning, paprika and stock and simmer gently until the meat is cooked—about 35 minutes.
7. Add breadcrumbs and extra stock if necessary.

8 Pour into the bread case, replace the lid and leave to get cold.
9 To serve, cut the loaf down in slices using a sharp knife.

Beef roll

cooking time about 1 hour

you will need:

1 lb. stewing beef
4 oz. fat bacon
3 - 4 cooked potatoes
salt, pepper
1 tablespoon chutney
1 tablespoon horseradish cream (see page 78)
1 beaten egg
dripping

1 Mince beef and bacon.
2 Mash potatoes and mix well with the meat.
3 Add seasoning and flavourings and mix thoroughly.
4 Bind with the egg.
5 Turn on to a floured board and form into a compact roll.
6 Heat a little dripping in a baking tin, put roll in, baste with fat and cook in a hot oven for about 1 hour, basting frequently (450°F.—Gas Mark 7).
7 Leave to get quite cold before wrapping in foil or slicing to serve.

Glazed ham and beef loaf

cooking time 1½ hours

you will need:

1 lb. raw minced beef
4 oz. ham, chopped
2 teaspoons chopped chives
1 teaspoon chopped parsley
salt, freshly ground black pepper
4 oz. breadcrumbs
2 eggs, beaten

For the glaze:
¼ pint aspic jelly (made according to packet instructions)
3 tablespoons mayonnaise (see page 79)
gherkin, olives, radishes, etc. to decorate

1 Mix the meat, flavourings, seasoning and breadcrumbs together.
2 Mix all well and bind with the eggs.
3 Put into a greased tin or pudding basin, cover with greased paper or foil and steam for 1½ hours.
4 Leave for a few minutes before turning out, then leave to cool.

To make the glaze:

5 When aspic jelly is cold but not set, stir in mayonnaise.
6 Leave until thick enough to coat the back of a spoon, then pour over the meat loaf, smooth it with a knife dipped in hot water.
7 Decorate and leave to get quite firm.

Salads and Moulds

Do not omit salads from a packed meal because of the difficulty of packing them. If you like a simple salad of lettuce, tomato, spring onions etc. prepare all the ingredients at home, washing the leafy vegetables under running water. Dry well and place in polythene bags. With salad dressing in a screw top jar, you can quickly assemble the salad on the spot. Put lettuce, etc. into a large polythene bag, add sliced tomatoes and cucumber, then watercress, and pour in the dressing.
Lightly shake the contents of the bag and serve the salad on picnic plates.

Made-up salads travel very well in a bowl covered with foil or a large polythene bag. Plastic bowls with 'seal on' lids are also excellent. All salads should be kept in a cool place, a refrigerator if possible, until the last minute before they are packed.
For a change and for ease of eating, try a moulded salad. These may be packed in the dish in which they are set and spooned out, or better still allowed to set in individual dishes. Cream or yoghourt containers are ideal for transport and the salad can be eaten from the container with a spoon.

Pineapple salad

you will need:

1 small fresh pineapple	mayonnaise (see page 79)
1 celery heart	lettuce leaves
	lemon slices

1. Peel and core the pineapple and shred finely.
2. Wash the celery, shred, then mix with the pineapple. Add enough mayonnaise to moisten.
3. Serve very cold, set in lettuce leaves and garnished with lemon.
4. Transport in waxed container or screw-top jar.

Beetroot salad

you will need:

2 small cooked beetroots	French dressing (see page 80)
grated horseradish	

1. Dice the beetroot and place in a bowl.
2. Sprinkle with freshly grated horseradish and pour on a little French dressing. Turn over once or twice and serve.
3. Transport in waxed container or screw-top jar.

Potato salad

you will need:

6 large new potatoes or waxy old potatoes	1 tablespoon chopped parsley
½ pint salad cream (see page 80)	seasoning
2 finely chopped spring onions or 1 heaped teaspoon chopped chives	radishes or tomatoes
	cress

1. Boil the potatoes in their jackets until just soft.
2. While hot, peel, dice neatly, and mix with the dressing, spring onions or chives, parsley, salt and pepper to taste.
3. Pile on to a dish and garnish with overlapping slices of radish or tomato, and cress.
4. Transport in a waxed container or a screw-top jar.

Celery and nut salad

you will need:

2 cooking apples or 2 oranges	mayonnaise or salad cream (see pages 79, 80)
4 oz. grapes	crisp lettuce leaves, cos if possible
1 large or 2 small celery hearts	walnut halves

1. Quarter the apples, core and cut into thin slices, or remove the skin and pith from the oranges and quarter.
2. Halve the grapes and remove pips. Wash the celery hearts and shred finely.
3. Mix all together lightly, with mayonnaise or salad dressing.
4. Line a plate with crisp, well-washed lettuce leaves, pile the salad in the centre and garnish with the walnuts.
5. Transport in a waxed container or a screw-top jar.

Chicken and mushroom moulds

cooking time about 2 minutes

you will need:

½ pint aspic jelly	¼ pint white sauce (see page 78)
1 small cucumber	8 oz. cooked chicken, diced
4 oz. mushrooms	salt, pepper
3-4 tablespoons milk	

1. Make aspic jelly according to packet instructions and put 1 spoonful into the bottom of each of 6 dariole moulds. Put a cucumber slice in the bottom and cover with another spoonful of aspic. Leave to set.
2. Dice remaining cucumber.
3. Chop the mushrooms and cook for a few minutes in the milk.
4. Add the remaining aspic jelly to the white sauce and mix well. Add the diced cucumber, mushrooms, chicken and seasoning.
5. Spoon into the prepared dariole moulds and leave to set.

Lobster and eggs in aspic

you will need:

1 can lobster	6 olives
1 pint aspic jelly make according to packet instructions)	2 hard-boiled eggs

1. Break the lobster into small pieces.
2. Put a spoonful of cold liquid aspic into the bottom of 8 dariole moulds, decorate with a few slices of olive, cover with a little more aspic and leave to set.
3. Fill the moulds with alternate layers of lobster and sliced egg.
4. Cover with a layer of aspic jelly and leave in the refrigerator or a cool place to set.

Tuna moulds

you will need:

1 8-oz. can tuna fish
2 eggs
¼ pint white sauce (see page 78)
2 level teaspoons gelatine
⅛ pint hot water
1 tablespoon vinegar
salt, pepper
2 tablespoons cream

1 Flake fish finely with a fork.
2 Separate the eggs and add the beaten yolks to the white sauce.
3 Dissolve the gelatine in the hot water, add the vinegar and stir into the sauce.
4 Add the fish, seasoning and cream and finally fold in the stiffly beaten egg whites.
5 Put into dariole moulds or waxed cartons and leave to set.

Eggs in aspic

you will need:

½ pint aspic jelly
4 - 5 hard-boiled eggs

1 Make the aspic jelly according to instructions on the packet and leave to get cold.
2 Into the bottom of 6 - 8 dariole moulds put 1 tablespoon jelly and 1 slice egg. When set, put another spoonful of jelly on top and leave to get quite firm.
3 Fill moulds with slices of egg and cover with cold, but still liquid aspic jelly. Leave to set.

Chicken mayonnaise

you will need:

12 oz. cooked chicken
8 oz. celery
2 dessert apples
2 heaped tablespoons walnuts
½ pint (approx.) mayonnaise (see page 79)
lettuce

1 Chop chicken, celery, apples and walnuts.
2 Toss lightly and mix with mayonnaise.
3 Line salad container with lettuce and fill with chicken mixture.

Fish mould

cooking time 1 hour

you will need:

1 lb. cooked white fish
½ pint shrimps
½ pint prawns
½ pint white sauce (see page 78)
1 teaspoon lemon juice
1 tablespoon anchovy essence
2 eggs, separated
salt and pepper
few drops cochineal

1 Flake the fish finely, removing all skin and bones.
2 Add the shrimps and the prawns cut into small pieces.
3 Add the sauce, lemon juice, anchovy essence and egg yolks and season carefully.
4 Beat the egg whites stiffly and fold into mixture. Improve the colour with 1 or 2 drops of cochineal.
5 Put into a buttered mould or pudding basin, cover with buttered paper and steam for 1 hour.
6 When quite cold, the mould should be transported in the basin in which it was cooked.

Beetroot jelly

cooking time about 3 minutes

you will need:

1 packet raspberry, cherry or red plum jelly
¾ pint water
¼ pint vinegar
1 cooked beetroot, diced

1 Put the jelly tablet into a pan with the water and heat gently until the jelly has dissolved.
2 Remove from the heat and stir vinegar in.
3 When beginning to set, stir in the beetroot.
4 Spoon into dariole cups or small waxed containers and leave to set.

This is served with cold boiled bacon (see page 84) or ham.

Jellied vegetable salad

you will need:

1 packet lime or lemon jelly
2 tablespoons lemon juice
water
1 cup diced celery
1 cup grated carrot
2 tablespoons cooked green peas

1 Put the jelly tablet into a measuring jug, add the lemon juice and enough hot water to make 1 pint. Stir until the jelly has dissolved.
2 Leave until beginning to set, then stir in the vegetables.
3 Spoon into dariole moulds or small waxed containers.
4 Leave to set.

Vegetable jellies

you will need:

- 1 level tablespoon gelatine
- ¾ pint strained chicken stock, hot
- 2 tablespoons tomato juice
- 1 tablespoon lemon juice
- ⅛ pint vinegar
- 1 teaspoon sugar
- seasoning
- 6 oz. cooked green peas
- 6 oz. diced cooked carrots
- 3 oz. thinly shredded cabbage
- 3 oz. diced cucumber

1. Dissolve the gelatine in the hot stock.
2. Add tomato juice, lemon juice, vinegar and sugar.
3. Add seasoning carefully, dependent on the stock used.
4. Leave to get cold and, when it begins to thicken, stir in vegetables, distributing them as evenly as possible.
5. Pour into wetted dariole moulds or into small waxed containers and leave to set.

Excellent to serve with cold ham, chicken or galantine (see page 56).

Tomato jelly

cooking time about 20 minutes

you will need:

- 1 lb. tomatoes, peeled, seeded and chopped
- 2 small onions, peeled and chopped
- 1 small clove garlic, crushed
- 1 bay leaf
- 6 peppercorns
- ½ level teaspoon salt
- pinch celery salt
- grated nutmeg
- 1 level teaspoon sugar
- 1 level tablespoon gelatine
- little hot water
- 1 tablespoon tarragon vinegar
- 3 tablespoons lemon juice
- cochineal (optional)

1. Put the tomatoes, onions and garlic together into a pan.
2. Add the bay leaf and peppercorns tied in muslin.
3. Add the salt, the celery salt, nutmeg and sugar, and cook altogether slowly until onion is quite tender.
4. Remove the bay leaf and peppercorns and add the gelatine dissolved in a little hot water.
5. Add vinegar and lemon juice and a little water if necessary to make the quantity up to 1 pint.
6. Check the seasoning then add a few drops of cochineal.
7. Pour into dariole tins and leave to set.

Serve with chicken mayonnaise (see page 61) or cold meats.

Crab salad

you will need:

- 1 lettuce
- 1 bunch watercress
- 3 - 4 firm tomatoes
- 1 small can crab or 1 fresh crab
- 3 - 4 cooked new potatoes, diced
- mayonnaise (see page 79)

1. Arrange the lettuce and watercress in a salad bowl and surround with thin tomato wedges.
2. Mix the crab meat and potatoes together and add enough mayonnaise to moisten.
3. Pile on top of the lettuce.
4. Cover bowl with foil, leave in a cool place until required.

Egg salad

you will need:

- 1 lettuce
- 3 hard-boiled eggs
- few radishes
- 5 - 6 tablespoons mayonnaise (see page 79)
- 5 - 6 sardines or anchovies
- watercress or mustard and cress

1. Prepare the lettuce and put into a fairly shallow salad bowl.
2. Cut the eggs in half lengthwise and arrange on the lettuce cut-side downwards.
3. Coat each with mayonnaise.
4. Cut the anchovies or sardines into fillets and use with the radishes and cress to garnish.
5. Cover salad bowl with foil, leave in a cool place until required.

Celery and cream cheese salad

you will need:

- 1 lettuce
- 1 - 2 heads celery
- 4 oz. cream cheese
- 2 tablespoons salad oil
- 1 tablespoons lemon juice
- salt and pepper
- 1 - 2 gherkins
- chopped nuts (optional)

1. Arrange the lettuce in a salad bowl.
2. Cut the celery into strips and pile on top of the lettuce.
3. Mix the cream cheese with the oil and lemon juice. Add salt and pepper and chopped gherkins.
4. Pour over the celery and decorate with chopped nuts.

Fruit and cheese salad

you will need:

- 1 carton cottage cheese
- 2 oz. walnuts, chopped
- 1 - 2 rings pineapple
- 1 lettuce
- 1 grapefruit
- 2 bananas
- French dressing (see page 80)

1 Mix the cheese with the nuts and pineapple.
2 Arrange the lettuce on a shallow dish, reserving the heart for decorating.
3 Pile the cheese in the centre.
4 Arrange the segments of grapefruit and slices of banana around the cheese, interspersed with pieces of the lettuce heart.
5 Pour the dressing over the top.

Salad Niçoise

you will need:

½ small clove garlic
½ lettuce
1 head chicory
2 tomatoes, peeled and quartered
small piece cucumber, sliced
2 hard-boiled eggs, sliced
1 7 oz. can tuna
French dressing (see page 80)
1 small can anchovy fillets
few black olives (optional)

1 Rub the salad bowl with the cut clove of garlic.
2 Shred the lettuce, divide the spears of chicory and put into the salad bowl with the tomatoes, cucumber and eggs.
3 Drain excess oil from the fish, divide into 4 portions and put on top of the salad.
4 Pour dressing over and garnish with anchovy fillets and olives.
5 Cover the top of the bowl with foil, leave in a cool place until required.

Cabbage and celery slaw

you will need:

4 oz. shredded raw cabbage
2 oz. shredded celery
2 oz. cooked potato
2 teaspoons minced onion
mayonnaise (see page 79)

1 Mix all the vegetables together and add enough mayonnaise to bind.
2 Toss lightly together and put into a salad container.

Cream cheese and orange salad

you will need:

1 lettuce
1 bunch watercress
small piece cucumber
2 - 3 oranges
few grapes
1 carton cottage cheese
2 oz. chopped nuts
French dressing (see page 80)

1 Arrange the lettuce, watercress and sliced cucumber in a salad bowl.
2 Peel the oranges, dice and put in a circle with the grapes.
3 Mix the cheese with the nuts, roll into balls and arrange with the other ingredients.
4 Add the dressing just before serving.

Tasmanian salad

you will need:

small piece of cucumber
2 - 3 celery sticks
2 dessert apples
2 bananas
lemon juice
4 tomatoes
salt and pepper
French dressing (see page 80)
lettuce

1 Dice the cucumber and celery.
2 Peel and slice the apples and bananas and sprinkle with lemon juice.
3 Slice the tomatoes and sprinkle with salt and pepper.
4 Mix all the ingredients together and pour a little salad dressing over.
5 Arrange the lettuce in a salad container and pile the mixture on top.

Tomato salad

you will need:

1 lb. firm tomatoes
pinch sugar
2 spring onions or a little chopped onion
French dressing (see page 80)
chopped parsley

1 Peel and slice the tomatoes and arrange on a flat serving dish. Add the sugar.
2 Sprinkle with the onion and pour the dressing over.
3 Sprinkle with parsley before serving.

Cucumber salad

you will need:

½ large or 1 small cucumber
salt
2 tablespoons French dressing (see page 80)
1 teaspoon finely chopped parsley

1 The cucumber can be peeled or not as preferred. Slice thinly, put on to a dish and sprinkle with salt. Leave to stand for an hour, if possible, then drain off surplus water.
2 Arrange cucumber on a picnic plate, pour the dressing over and sprinkle with parsley.

Russian salad

you will need:

- 1 - 2 cooked carrots, diced
- 1 - 2 cooked potatoes, diced
- 2 tablespoons cooked green peas
- 2 tablespoons cooked French beans, cut into pieces
- ½ small cooked beetroot
- mayonnaise (see page 79)
- 1 gherkin, chopped
- 3 - 4 anchovy fillets

1 Put all the vegetables together in a bowl.
2 Add enough mayonnaise to moisten well.
3 Put into a salad container and garnish with gherkin and the anchovy fillets.

Portuguese salad

you will need:

- 1 can tuna
- 3 - 4 olives
- lemon juice
- pepper
- 8 oz. cooked new potatoes — sliced
- 8 oz. cooked French beans
- 3 - 4 tomatoes, peeled and sliced
- 1 head chicory

For the dressing:

- 1 level teaspoon dry mustard
- 1 tablespoon white vinegar
- 2 tablespoons oil
- salt and pepper

1 Drain excess oil from the fish, flake finely and mix with the chopped olives. Add lemon juice and pepper to taste.
2 Arrange the potatoes, beans and tomatoes in layers on a serving dish.
3 Pile the fish on top.
4 Mix the mustard smoothly with the vinegar, add the oil and seasoning and pour this dressing over the fish.
5 Divide the chicory into spears and use to garnish the salad.

Salad Palermo

you will need:

- 1 small lettuce
- 2 tablespoons diced cooked carrots
- 2 tablespoons cooked green peas
- 2 tablespoons cooked rice
- salt and pepper
- 1 good tablespoon mayonnaise (see page 79)
- lemon juice
- little made mustard
- 4 - 6 slices cooked ham
- olives
- tomatoes

1 Line a shallow serving dish with the lettuce.
2 Mix the carrots, peas and rice together, and season as required.
3 Mix the mayonnaise with a squeeze of lemon juice and a little mustard.
4 Add the vegetables to the mayonnaise and mix well.
5 Put a good spoonful of the mixture on each slice of ham and roll up or just fold over.
6 Arrange on the lettuce and garnish with olives or wedges of tomato.

Pineapple and lettuce salad

you will need:

- 1 lettuce
- 3 tablespoons oil
- 1 tablespoon vinegar
- 1 tablespoon pineapple juice
- salt and pepper
- pinch sugar
- ½ small can pineapple
- 2 teaspoons finely chopped parsley

1 Prepare and shred the lettuce.
2 Mix the oil, vinegar, pineapple juice, seasoning and sugar together, toss the lettuce in it, then remove and arrange around the edge of a salad bowl.
3 Dice the pineapple and put into the centre of the bowl.
4 Add the parsley to the remaining dressing and pour over the pineapple.

Beetroot baskets

you will need:

- 4 medium-sized beetroots, cooked and left whole
- 1 teaspoon chopped chives
- 1 level teaspoon chopped mint
- 1 tablespoon finely diced cooked potatoes
- 1 tablespoon chopped pickled walnuts
- mayonnaise or salad cream (see page 79)

1 Cut a slice from the top of each beetroot and, with a small teaspoon, scoop out the centre.
2 Chop the scooped-out beetroot and mix with the other ingredients.
3 Bind with a little mayonnaise, then pile into beetroot cases.
4 Wrap each in foil or greaseproof paper and pack in a container.

Bean and apple salad

you will need:

- 4 oz. cooked broad beans
- 1 small dessert apple, sliced finely
- 2-3 tablespoons raw white cabbage, shredded
- salt
- 4 tablespoons mayonnaise or salad cream (see page 79)
- 1 hard-boiled egg
- 1-2 pickled walnuts

1 Mix the beans with the apple and cabbage and season with a little salt.
2 Put into a salad container and coat with the mayonnaise.
3 Garnish with sliced egg and walnuts.

Apple and carrot salad

you will need:

- lettuce
- 2 dessert apples
- 2-3 raw carrots
- 1 tablespoon seedless raisins
- 2 tablespoons cream
- 2 teaspoons lemon juice
- salt and pepper

1 Prepare enough lettuce to line a small shallow salad bowl.
2 Chop the apple, grate the carrots and add the raisins.
3 Half whip the cream, add lemon juice and seasoning.
4 Add the apple mixture, blend lightly together and serve on the bed of lettuce.

Moulded grapefruit salad

you will need:

- 1 16 oz. can grapefruit
- ½ oz. gelatine
- 2 tablespoons lemon juice
- 1 dessert apple, peeled, cored and chopped
- 2-3 sticks celery, chopped

1 Drain the syrup from the grapefruit and make the quantity up to ½ pint with water.
2 Dissolve the gelatine in a little of the syrup, over hot water, then add to the rest of the syrup. Add lemon juice and leave until it begins to thicken.
3 Fold in the grapefruit segments, apple and celery.
4 Pour into a mould and turn out when required.

Note

This salad is very good served with chicken, ham or veal.

Honeyed salad

you will need:

For the dressing:

- 1 tablespoon thin honey
- 2 tablespoons lemon juice
- 8 oz. dessert apples
- 2 oz. seedless raisins
- 8 oz. cooked carrots

1 Mix the honey and lemon juice together.
2 Peel, core and dice the apples.
3 Add the raisins, chopped nuts and sliced carrots.
4 Mix with the dressing and leave in a cool place for an hour before using.

Note

Serve this salad with galantine (see page 56) or cold chicken.

Salmon and shrimp mayonnaise

you will need:

- 1 small can salmon
- 1 4 oz. can shrimps
- small piece cucumber
- 2-3 tomatoes
- mayonnaise (see page 79)
- lettuce

1 Flake the salmon and add the shrimps, reserving a few for garnish.
2 Slice the cucumber and tomatoes.
3 Mix some mayonnaise with the fish and place in the centre of a serving dish lined with lettuce.
4 Arrange alternate slices of cucumber and tomato around the edge and use the remaining shrimps to garnish the fish.
5 Serve extra mayonnaise separately.

Salmon cole slaw

you will need:

- 1 7 oz. can salmon
- ½ small cucumber, peeled and diced
- 3 tablespoons salad cream (see page 79)
- lemon juice
- pepper and salt
- 1 small or ½ firm Savoy cabbage
- 2 hard-boiled eggs
- 2 tomatoes

1 Flake the salmon, add cucumber and salad cream.
2 Season with lemon juice, pepper and salt as required.
3 Shred the cabbage and put into a serving dish.
4 Pile the fish on top and garnish with egg slices and wedges of tomatoes.

Soups

In each case the stock can be made with chicken or beef stock cubes and extra seasoning may not be necessary.

A *bouquet garni* is a bunch of fresh herbs for flavouring and usually consists of 1 bay leaf, 1 sprig thyme and parsley, tied with thread. A small piece celery may be included. With thread long enough to hang over the edge of the pan, the *bouquet* is easily removed before serving.

Consommé

cooking time about 10 minutes

you will need for 4 servings:

1½ pints chicken stock
2 tablespoons sherry
squeeze lemon juice
salt and pepper

1 Heat the stock.
2 Add sherry and lemon juice.
3 Add seasoning as required.
4 Serve with croûtons, or sprinkle with parsley.

To make croûtons:

1 Dice some day-old bread or cut into fancy shapes, then fry in hot fat. Drain well.
2 Or make some toast and cut into dice.

Consommé à la princesse

cooking time about 10 minutes

you will need for 4 servings:

4 oz. cooked chicken
1½ pints chicken stock
4 oz. cooked green peas
salt and pepper

1 Shred the chicken.
2 Put into a pan with stock and peas, heat well.
3 Add seasoning as required.

Jellied consommé

cooking time about 15 minutes

you will need for 4 servings:

2 pints chicken stock
½ oz. gelatine
2 tablespoons sherry
1 tablespoon lemon juice
1 egg white
1 egg shell, crushed

1 Put all the ingredients together in a large pan.
2 Heat to boiling point, whisking all the time.
3 Simmer for 5 minutes, then strain through a piece of double muslin.
4 Season as necessary and leave to set.
5 Break up with a fork and serve well chilled.

Tomato consommé

Follow the recipe as above and add 1 small can tomato purée to the other ingredients.

Vichyssoise soup

cooking time about 30 minutes

you will need for 4 servings:

8 oz. potatoes
1 leek
6 spring onions
8 oz. green peas
sprig fresh mint
1½ pints chicken stock
salt and pepper
½ oz. cornflour
½ pint milk
½ oz. butter
¼ pint thin cream

1 Prepare and chop the potatoes, leek and spring onions. Put into a pan with peas, mint, stock and seasoning.
2 Simmer until tender, then rub through a sieve.
3 Mix the cornflour smoothly with a little of the milk. Put the rest on to heat with the butter.
4 Add to the mixed cornflour and stir until boiling.
5 Add this sauce to the purée and mix well.
6 Correct the seasoning and add the cream.
7 Chill thoroughly.

Potato and leek soup

cooking time about 25 minutes

you will need for 4 servings:

1 bacon rasher
1 oz. butter
1 lb. potatoes
3 leeks
1 pint stock or water
salt and pepper
2-3 tablespoons thin cream or top of the milk
parsley
cheese

1 Chop the bacon and fry lightly.
2 Add the butter.

3 Chop the potatoes and leeks and sauté in the fat for a few minutes.
4 Add the stock, salt and pepper.
5 Cover and simmer for about 20 minutes.
6 Add the cream.
7 Just before serving, add chopped parsley and serve with grated cheese.

Onion soup

cooking time about 30 minutes

you will need for 4 servings:

1 lb. onions
1 oz. butter
¾ pint stock
bouquet garni (see page 66)
2 level tablespoons flour
¼ pint milk
3 - 4 tablespoons croûtons (see page 66)
grated cheese

1 Slice the onions thinly and cook slowly in the butter until tender.
2 Add the stock and *bouquet garni.*
3 Cover and simmer for about 20 minutes.
4 Mix the flour smoothly with the milk and stir into the soup.
5 Stir until boiling and boil for 1 minute.
6 Season as required.
7 Put croûtons into a tureen, pour soup over.
8 Sprinkle with cheese or serve it separately.

Watercress soup

cooking time about 30 minutes

you will need for 4 servings:

2 bundles watercress
1 oz. butter
1 pint chicken stock
½ oz. flour
¼ pint milk
salt and pepper
3 tablespoons single cream
green food colouring (optional)

1 Wash the watercress and chop coarsely, keeping some sprigs for garnish.
2 Melt the butter and sauté the watercress for a few minutes.
3 Add the stock and simmer for about 15 minutes.
4 Rub through a sieve and return to the pan.
5 Mix the flour smoothly with the milk, add to the purée and stir until boiling.
6 Simmer for 3 minutes. Correct the seasoning.
7 Just before serving, add the cream and a few drops of green food colouring.
8 Garnish with sprigs of watercress.

Summer soup

cooking time about 25 minutes

you will need for 4 servings:

2 pints stock or water
2 oz. sago
3 - 4 carrots
2 - 3 oz. runner beans
1 small onion
½ small lettuce
1 sprig mint
8 oz. green peas
salt and pepper

1 Heat the stock to boiling point, add the sago.
2 Dice the carrots and beans, chop the onion finely.
3 Shred the lettuce and chop the mint.
4 Add all the ingredients to the pan with a little salt and pepper.
5 Cover and simmer until the vegetables are tender and the sago is cooked.

Tomato soup

cooking time about 1½ hours

you will need for 4 servings:

1 lb. fresh or canned tomatoes
1 onion
1 carrot
½ oz. butter
1 oz. bacon scraps, chopped
1 pint stock or juice from canned tomatoes
grated nutmeg
lemon juice
bouquet garni (see page 66)
cornflour
milk
salt and pepper
sugar
chopped chives

1 Slice the tomatoes, onion and carrot. If canned tomatoes are used, strain them and make the juice up to 1 pint with stock.
2 Melt the butter in a deep pan and lightly fry the sliced vegetables and bacon for 10 minutes.
3 Boil the stock or tomato juice and add to the vegetables with the nutmeg, lemon juice and *bouquet garni* and cook for 45 minutes - 1 hour until tender.
4 Press through a nylon sieve using a wooden spoon. Measure purée and thicken, allowing ½ oz. cornflour blended with a little cold milk to each pint.
5 Stir in the cornflour, bring slowly to the boil, stirring. Allow to cook for 2 - 3 minutes.
6 Season to taste with salt, pepper and a little sugar.
7 To serve, sprinkle with chives.

Chicken and celery soup

cooking time — about 20 minutes

you will need for 4 servings:

4 oz. celery
1½ pints chicken stock
4 oz. cooked chicken
1 oz. flour
1 egg
½ pint milk
salt and pepper
grated cheese

1. Chop the celery into small pieces. Cook in the stock until tender.
2. Dice the chicken and add to the stock.
3. Mix the flour, egg and milk together smoothly and stir into the other ingredients.
4. Heat carefully until the soup thickens.
5. Correct the seasoning and serve with the cheese.

Lemon soup

cooking time — 15 – 20 minutes

you will need for 4 servings:

2 egg yolks
½ oz. cornflour
1½ pints chicken stock or water
juice ½ lemon
¼ pint cream
2 oz. cooked rice
½ oz. toasted shredded almonds

1. Mix the egg yolks and cornflour with a little of the cold stock or water.
2. Add to the remaining stock, heat gently to boiling point, then simmer for 3 minutes, stirring all the time.
3. Cool, then add lemon juice, cream and rice.
4. Chill thoroughly and serve sprinkled with almonds.

Clam soup

cooking time — 15 – 20 minutes

you will need for 4 servings:

1 oz. butter
little grated onion
1 oz. flour
½ pint white stock
½ pint milk
1 7½ oz. can minced clams
salt and pepper
pinch celery salt
little chopped parsley
grated cheese

1. Melt the butter and sauté the onion for a few minutes.
2. Add the flour and mix well, cook for a few minutes longer.
3. Add the stock and milk gradually. Stir until boiling and boil for 1 minute.
4. Add the clams and reheat without boiling.
5. Add salts and pepper as required.
6. Sprinkle with parsley before serving and serve cheese separately.

Cucumber soup

cooking time — about 25 minutes

you will need for 4 servings:

1 large cucumber
6 spring onions
1½ pints chicken stock
1 oz. flour
little milk or water
salt and pepper
¼ pint thin cream
few drops green food colouring

1. Peel and chop cucumber, chop onions and simmer in the stock until the cucumber is tender.
2. Rub through a sieve then return to the pan.
3. Mix the flour smoothly with a little cold milk or water, add to the soup, stir until boiling and simmer for 3 minutes.
4. Season as required and add the cream.
5. Add a few drops of green colouring and chill thoroughly.

Dips

Some sandwich fillings make excellent 'dips' and are very much appreciated by those who feel that they should not eat too much bread. Small savoury biscuits or starch-reduced crisp breads may be used to dip into any of these mixtures.

For anyone really calorie conscious, raw vegetables — fingers of carrot or chunks of apple — may be used instead of biscuits. For a meal out of doors the dips can be easily carried in screw-top jars or waxed cartons. Dips improve if made the day before use, and are left in a cold place overnight.

Egg and curry dip

you will need:

- 3 hard-boiled eggs
- 4-5 tablespoons mayonnaise (see page 79)
- 1 tablespoon curry powder
- 1 tablespoon tomato ketchup
- salt, pepper

1 Mash the eggs well. It is easier if this is done before the eggs are quite cold.
2 Add all the other ingredients, mix well and season to taste.

Blue cheese dip

you will need:

- 8 oz. blue cheese
- 1½ oz. butter
- 4-5 tablespoons mayonnaise (see page 79)
- 1 egg yolk
- 2 tablespoons red wine
- thin cream or top of the milk
- 1 teaspoon chopped chives
- salt and pepper

1 Beat the cheese with a wooden spoon until it is quite creamy.
2 Soften the butter, and work it into the cheese.
3 Add the mayonnaise, egg yolk and wine and mix well together.
4 Add enough cream to give a soft consistency and finally add the chives. Season if necessary.

Fluellen's dip

you will need:

- 1 packet leek soup mix
- 2 cartons sour cream
- 2 oz. grated Parmesan cheese
- 1 oz. walnuts
- paprika pepper

1 Mix the soup smoothly with the cream.
2 Add grated cheese and chopped walnuts and a sprinkling of paprika.

Cheese and tomato dip

you will need:

- 1 tablespoon mayonnaise (see page 79)
- 1 tablespoon tomato ketchup
- 2-3 oz. packets cream cheese spread
- pinch salt
- pinch sugar

1 Mix the mayonnaise and ketchup together.
2 Beat the cheese with a wooden spoon until it is smooth and creamy.
3 Add the mayonnaise mixture a little at a time.
4 Add salt and sugar to taste.

Chilli dip

you will need:

- 2 oz. blue cheese
- 2 tablespoons chilli sauce (see page 78)
- 1 tablespoon dry Vermouth
- ¼ pint sour cream

1 Beat all ingredients together until smooth and creamy.

Cheese and horseradish dip

you will need:

- 6 oz. cream cheese
- 2-3 tablespoons mayonnaise (see page 79)
- 2 tablespoons chilli sauce (see page 78)
- 1 tablespoon horseradish cream
- 1 tablespoon chopped pickles

1 Beat the cheese till smooth and creamy.
2 Add the mayonnaise a little at a time until well blended.
3 Add the rest of the ingredients and mix all well together.

Avocado and tomato dip

you will need:

- 1 ripe avocado
- 1 tablespoon lemon juice
- 1 tablespoon white wine vinegar
- 1 tomato, peeled, seeded and chopped
- ½ small onion, peeled and finely chopped
- 1-2 drops Tabasco sauce
- ½ teaspoon Worcestershire sauce
- pinch pepper
- pinch salt

1 Peel and stone the avocado and rub through a sieve.
2 Add lemon juice and vinegar and then all the other ingredients.
3 Cover at once or the dip will begin to discolour.

Confetti dip

you will need:

- ½ packet leek soup mix
- ½ pint sour cream
- 2 tablespoons peeled, chopped cucumber
- 2 tablespoons chopped green pepper
- 2 tablespoons finely chopped pimento

1 Mix all ingredients together and chill until required.

Onion dip

you will need:

- ¼ pint yoghourt
- 8 oz. cottage cheese
- 3 - 4 tablespoons mayonnaise (see page 79)
- ½ packet onion soup mix
- 1 tablespoon chopped parsley

1 Mix the yoghourt and cottage cheese together.
2 Add mayonnaise and mix in well.
3 Add soup mix and parsley and stir till all ingredients are well blended.
4 Chill until required.

Cucumber dip

you will need:

- 4 oz. cream cheese
- ¼ pint sour cream
- few drops vinegar
- 1 teaspoon celery salt
- 1 tablespoon chopped chives
- ½ cucumber, peeled and finely chopped

1 Beat the cream cheese till soft and smooth and add the sour cream.
2 Add vinegar, celery salt and chives.
3 Fold in the cucumber, and chill until required.

Hot and Cold Drinks

There is really no limit to the beverages that are possible for a packed meal, provided that one has a suitable container to make them portable.

Soft drinks are best carried in their own bottles. If possible chill well before packing. A bottle taken from the fridge and wrapped in newspaper will keep cold for about 4 hours. If you eat out of doors frequently and are using a car for transport, it is worth investing in a large, wide-necked flask which can be used for ice. If the family's taste involves taking a variety of cold drinks, line a plastic bucket with newspaper, pack the bottles in this, top with sheets of newspaper, well tucked in around the bottles and thus insulated, the 'bar' will travel very well.

Hot tea or coffee should be made by the usual method and, although milk may be added, the flavour is considered to be much better if the milk is packed separately. Pour into a flask or jug which has been well rinsed out in hot water for a hot drink or cold water for a cold drink. Remember that drinks will keep hot longer (about 3 hours) if the flask is full.

All types of flasks should be stored, when not in use, upside down without the cork or lid. Always make sure that the flask and cork are washed and thoroughly dried before putting them away.

Iced tea

Make strong tea using 1 teaspoon tea leaves per person.

Strain into a jug and chill.

Serve poured over ice cubes, with a thin slice of lemon or orange added.

Garnish with a sprig of mint, if available.

Coffee

The jug method is the easiest and one of the best ways of making coffee.

For every pint of water you need 2 heaped tablespoons coffee (fine ground).

1 Heat jug by filling it with boiling water and allowing to stand about 5 minutes.
2 Empty the jug and dry it.
3 Put coffee in the jug and pour on the boiling water stirring vigorously.
4 Leave jug in a warm place for 5 minutes, stirring once or twice.
5 Leave without stirring for a further 5 minutes. The coffee is then ready to serve. If there appear to be too many grounds on the top, lightly skim these off with a spoon or carefully pour off one cup of coffee and then pour back into jug. This will make the grounds settle.

If you are serving the coffee in another pot, make sure that the pot is really hot. If it is necessary to reheat the coffee, take care that it does not boil.

Serve black or with warm milk, or thin cream.

Iced coffee

you will need:

¾ pint milk
4-6 oz. sugar
2 pints strong black coffee
vanilla essence
¼ pint thin cream

1 Put milk into a pan with the sugar and heat until sugar has dissolved; do not allow to boil.
2 Add coffee and a few drops of vanilla essence.
3 Strain and, when cool, add the cream.
4 Put into the refrigerator and chill thoroughly before putting into a vacuum flask.

Fruit juice appetiser

you will need:

½ pint orange juice
¼ pint lemon juice
¼ pint pineapple juice
2 oz. sugar
1 level teaspoon very finely chopped, fresh mint
1-2 tablespoons Cointreau (optional)

1 Mix all ingredients together and chill for at least 1 hour before pouring into a vacuum flask.

Lemonade

you will need:

3 large lemons
12 oz. sugar
1 oz. cream of tartar
3 quarts boiling water

1 Wash the lemons and peel them very thinly. A potato peeler is useful for this.
2 Put the peel into a large jug with the sugar and cream of tartar, and pour on the boiling water.
3 Stir until the sugar has dissolved, then cover and leave to cool.
4 Add the lemon juice, strain, and chill thoroughly before pouring into a vacuum flask.

Orangeade

you will need:

6 oranges
4 lemons
1¼ lb. sugar
4 pints water

1 Wash the fruit and peel thinly. Use a potato peeler as suggested for lemonade and be sure the peel is free from pith.
2 Put the rind with the sugar and 2 pints water, bring to boiling point and simmer for 10 minutes. Then strain and leave to get cold.
3 Add the fruit juice and remaining water and strain again.
4 Chill thoroughly before pouring into the vacuum flask.

Tomato juice cocktail

you will need:

1 pint tomato juice, fresh or canned
1 teaspoon Worcestershire sauce
1 tablespoon lemon juice
few drops of Tabasco sauce

1 Mix all the ingredients together and chill thoroughly before putting into the vacuum flask for transportation.

Recipes for reference

Breads

Quick wheatmeal loaves and rolls

cooking time 1 hour, including rising

you will need:

- 12 oz. each brown and white plain flours (or any proportion you like)
- 3 level teaspoons each, sugar and salt
- 1 oz. fresh yeast or ½ oz. dried yeast (1 level tablespoon)
- ¾ pint water

1 Mixing

To make dough with fresh yeast:

Mix the flours, salt and sugar together. Blend yeast in the water and add all at once. Mix to a soft, scone-like dough (adding more flour if necessary) that leaves the bowl clean.

To make dough with dried yeast:

Dissolve a teaspoon of the sugar in a cupful of warm water (from recipe quantity) then sprinkle dried yeast on top. Leave until frothy (10 - 15 minutes). Add, with rest of liquid, to flours, salt and remaining sugar. Mix to a soft, scone-like dough.

2 Shaping (to make 18 rolls):

Turn dough on to board. Flatten to ½-inch thickness. Cut into rounds with a 2½-inch cutter, or divide dough into 18 equal pieces and roll each piece to a ball, using palm of one hand. Press down hard at first then ease up. This is best done on an unfloured board with a little flour on palm of hand only. Place rolls on floured, ungreased baking sheet.

For soft-sided rolls which you pull apart, pack ¼ inch apart and dust with flour.

For crusty rolls, leave 1 inch space all round, brush tops with salt and water and sprinkle with cracked wheat or cornflakes.

3 Put the tray of rolls inside an oiled polythene bag and leave to rise until the rolls are double in size (see note on rising). Bake towards top of oven at 450°F.—Gas Mark 8 for 20 - 30 minutes.

To make three flower-pot loaves:

Divide the dough into 3 equal parts. Grease very thoroughly the inside of three 4- or 5-inch flower pots and shape a piece of dough to half fill each of them. Brush the tops with salt and water and sprinkle with cornflakes or cracked wheat. Put to rise, inside oiled polythene bags, until the dough has doubled in size and springs back when lightly pressed with a floured finger. Remove bags, bake at centre of oven 450°F.—Gas Mark 8 for 30 - 40 minutes.

To make two tin loaves:

Divide the dough in half, and shape each piece to fit the well-greased 1-lb. loaf tins. Rise and bake as for flower-pot loaves.

Note

Rising times can be varied to suit your own convenience.

Quick rise — ½ hour in a warm place.
Slower rise — 1-1½ hours on kitchen table.
Overnight rise — up to 12 hours in a cold larder.

Surplus dough can be kept in a refrigerator in a loosely tied polythene bag, or plastic pot with lid, for use next day or the day after.
To use refrigerated dough, soften by standing in a warm place for 15 - 20 minutes, then shape rolls or loaves from cold dough.
Cool or cold rising makes a stronger dough and therefore better bread.

Fruit breads with quick wheatmeal dough

Use this basic wheatmeal dough to make any of the following fruit breads. Choose the variety you like as the method is the same for each one. Surplus dough can be used to make rolls.

cooking time approximately 40 minutes

you will need:

- 8 oz. each brown and white plain flours
- 2 level teaspoons each sugar and salt
- ½ oz. fresh yeast or 2 level teaspoons dried yeast
- ½ pint water

To make dough with fresh yeast:
Mix the flours, salt and sugar together. Blend yeast in the water and add all at once. Mix to a soft scone-like dough (adding more flour if necessary) that leaves the bowl clean.

To make dough with dried yeast:
Dissolve a teaspoon of the sugar in a cupful of warm water (from recipe quantity), then sprinkle dried yeast on top. Leave until frothy (10 - 15 minutes). Add, with rest of liquid, to flours, salt and remaining sugar. Mix to a soft scone-like dough. Put the dough into an oiled, lightly tied polythene bag or container with lid, and allow to rise to double-size before using.

TO MAKE THE LOAVES: Choose a loaf and topping from one of the recipes below and use the following method.

1 Squeeze and work all the ingredients together in a basin, with one hand, until the mixture is no longer streaky.
2 Two-thirds fill the prepared tins (bottom-lined and greased) and put inside a polythene bag until dough rises to within ½ inch of the top of the tins. 1 hour in a warm place, longer in a cool one.
3 Cover with one of the toppings.
4 Bake on middle shelf of oven.
Fig and treacle bread
400°F.—Gas Mark 6, 45 - 50 mins.
Ginger loaf
400°F.—Gas Mark 6, 30 - 40 mins.
Apricot and walnut bread
450°F.—Gas Mark 8, 30 - 40 mins.
5 Cool in the tin for 10 minutes, then turn out on to a wire tray.

Fig and treacle bread

This bread supplies iron for vitality. Try a slice with a glass of orange juice at elevenses, or with a cup of hot milk at bedtime.

- 1½ lb. risen Quick Wheatmeal dough
- 8 oz. black treacle (approximately 6 tablespoons)
- 8 oz. figs, chopped
- 4 oz. brown sugar
- 2 oz. margarine

Makes two 1 lb. loaves or two 5-inch square tins.

Ginger loaf

This recipe is for a Ginger loaf not a Ginger cake. It is moist, dark and spicy and improves with keeping for 2 - 3 days. It should be eaten buttered, like bread, and is particularly good with the milder cheeses.

- 1 lb. risen Quick Wheatmeal dough
- 2 oz. black treacle (2 tablespoons)
- 1 oz. margarine or 2 tablespoons oil
- 1½ - 2 teaspoons ground ginger
- 2 oz. sultanas (optional)

Use 1 lb. loaf tin or 6-inch square tin.

Apricot and walnut loaf

This unusual fruit loaf is delicious with butter at tea time, or with cheese for supper.

- 12 oz. risen Quick Wheatmeal dough
- 4 oz. dried apricots, chopped
- 2 oz. broken walnuts
- 1 oz. sugar
- 1 oz. margarine

Makes 1 lb. loaf.

Toppings

1 Sprinkle with a crumble of 1 oz. butter, 1 oz. sugar, 1½ oz. plain flour rubbed together until it looks like coarse breadcrumbs.
2 Sprinkle crushed cornflakes on top of the dough.
3 After baking, brush the hot loaf with a wet brush dipped in honey or syrup.

Wholemeal bread

sufficient for 2 large or 4 small loaves

cooking time 30 – 40 minutes

you will need:

3 lb. wholemeal flour	1 pint water
2 level tablespoons each sugar and salt	
yeast liquid:	
blend 2 oz. fresh yeast in ½ pint water	or dissolve 1 teaspoon sugar in ½ pint warm water (110°F) and sprinkle 2 level tablespoons dried yeast on top. Leave till frothy (about 10 minutes)

1 Mix the dry ingredients with yeast liquid and sufficient of remaining water to make a firm dough that leaves the bowl clean.
2 Turn the dough on to a lightly floured board and knead, by folding dough towards you, then pushing down and away from you, with palm of hand. Give dough a quarter turn and repeat kneading, developing a rocking rhythm, until the dough feels firm and elastic and no longer sticky.
3 Shape the dough into a round ball and place in a closed container, such as a large oiled polythene bag, lightly tied, or an 8-inch oiled saucepan with lid, to keep it moist and prevent skinning. Stand the dough to rise until it doubles in size and springs back when pressed lightly with a floured finger.
4 When risen, turn the dough on to board and knead again until firm. Divide into 2 or 4, flatten each piece firmly with the knuckles to knock out air bubbles.
5 To make a tin loaf— shape each piece by folding in 3, or rolling up like a Swiss roll, and tuck in the ends.
The finally moulded pieces should exactly fit the tins (2 lb. or 1 lb.). Brush the tops with salted water and put each tin inside an oiled polythene bag (lightly tied). Put aside until the dough rises to the top of the tins (about 1 hour at room temperature).
6 Bake the loaves on the middle shelf of a hot oven 450°F.—Gas Mark 8 for 30 - 40 minutes, or until the loaves shrink from the sides of the tin.
7 Cool on a wire tray.
8 The loaves should be stored in an open polythene bag or a bread bin.

Variations

Divide each loaf piece into 5 smaller pieces, shape into rolls and fit into the tin.

Shape each piece of dough into a round cob, dust with flour, and put on to floured baking sheet and rise and bake.

Shape all the dough into a round cob, place on a large floured baking sheet. Cut into four, scatter with cracked wheat or flour, cover with oiled polythene and rise. Re-mark, if necessary, and bake at 450°F.—Gas Mark 8 for 40 - 45 minutes.

Malt bread

sufficient for two small loaves

cooking time 40 minutes approximately

you will need:

dry mix:	
1 lb. soft plain flour	6 oz. washed sultanas
1 level teaspoon salt	
yeast liquid:	
blend 1 oz. fresh yeast in ¼ pint + 2 tablespoons water	or dissolve 1 teaspoon sugar in ¼ pint + 3 tablespoons warm (110°F) water. Sprinkle on 1 tablespoon dried yeast. Leave until frothy (about 10 minutes)
additional ingredients:	
4 tablespoons malt extract (4 oz.)	1 tablespoon black treacle
	1 oz. margarine

1 Warm together malt extract, black treacle and margarine. Cool.
2 Add cooled liquid and yeast liquid to the dry mix and work to a soft dough that leaves the bowl clean.

Note

You may need a little extra flour for easy handling, but the dough should be as soft as possible. Turn on to a lightly floured board and knead, by stretching and folding, until the dough is smooth and elastic.

3 Divide in two, flatten each piece and roll up like a Swiss roll to fit the greased 1 lb. loaf tins. Put to rise in oiled polythene bags until

dough rises to the top of the tins and springs back when lightly pressed.
This loaf takes about 1¼ hours in a warm place, longer in a cool one.

4 Bake on middle shelf of oven at 400°F.—Gas Mark 6 for 40 - 45 mins.
5 Brush tops of hot loaves with a wet brush dipped in honey.
6 Cool on a wire tray.

Fruity tea bread

This quantity makes two small loaves

cooking time 30 – 40 minutes

you will need:

dry mix:

1 lb. strong plain flour
2 level teaspoons salt
1 oz. lard

yeast liquid:

blend 1½ oz. fresh yeast in ¼ pint water

or sprinkle 1½ tablespoons dried yeast on ¼ pint warm (110°F.) water. Leave till frothy (about 10 minutes)

additional ingredients:

1 tablespoon honey made up to ¼ pint liquid with warm milk
4 oz. each washed seedless raisins and currants
4 oz. mixed peel

1 Mix flour and salt, rub in hard and blend in all liquids at once. Work to a dough by squeezing with fingers until it leaves the bowl clean. Turn on to a lightly floured board and knead until dough feels smooth and elastic (about 5 minutes).
2 Put dough in an oiled polythene bag lightly tied or a greased saucepan with lid, and leave until dough doubles its size and springs back when lightly pressed with floured finger.
3 Turn on to board and work in the fruit. Divide the dough in two, flatten each piece and roll up like a Swiss roll to fit the greased 1 lb. loaf tins.
4 Place tins in oiled polythene bags and rise until dough reaches tops of tins.
5 Bake, on middle shelf of oven, at 380°F.—Gas Mark 5 for 30 - 40 minutes.
6 Brush tops of hot loaves with wet brush dipped in honey.
7 Cool on a wire tray.

Orange bread

sufficient for two small loaves

cooking time 30 minutes

you will need:

dry mix:

1 lb. strong plain flour
2 level teaspoons salt
1 oz. sugar

yeast liquid:

blend 1 oz. fresh yeast in ¼ pint water

or dissolve 1 teaspoon sugar in ¼ pint warm water (110°F.) and sprinkle 1 level tablespoon dried yeast on top. Leave till frothy (about 10 minutes)

additional ingredients:

1 egg — beaten
3 medium or 2 large 'shells' of orange minced or finely chopped to a pulp (6 oz.) OR the juice and rind of one whole orange

1 Mix all the ingredients with the yeast liquid.
2 Work to a firm dough (adding 3 - 4 tablespoons extra water if required), until the dough leaves the bowl clean.
3 Turn on to a lightly floured board, knead by pulling it up and pressing it down, until smooth and elastic.
4 Put the dough to rise inside an oiled polythene bag, lightly tied, or a large oiled pan or plastic storage jar with a lid, until it doubles in size and springs back when pressed with a floured finger.
5 Turn on to a floured board and knead lightly for 1 - 2 minutes. Divide into two. Flatten each piece and roll up like a Swiss roll, shaped to fit a 1 lb. bread tin.
6 Place the roll of dough in the greased bread tins. Put tins inside oiled polythene bags until the dough rises to the top of the tins.
7 Bake at 400°F.—Gas Mark 6 on the middle shelf of oven for 30 - 35 minutes.
8 Brush the baked bread with a wet brush dipped in honey or syrup.
9 Turn out and cool on a wire tray.

Orange bread is delicious, especially with cream cheese or chocolate spread, or toasted and eaten with marmalade or apricot jam. This recipe makes use of something often thrown away, i.e. the 'shells' of an orange after you have squeezed out the juice.

Orange treacle bread

1 Prepare and rise dough as in the previous recipe.
2 Add the treacle, and work in very well with one hand until the mix is an even brown and no longer streaky.
3 Pour into greased bread tin, rise, and continue as method for Orange bread.

Orange fruit bread

Add 6 oz. mixed cleaned dried fruit to the dry ingredients (stage 1) before mixing the dough in the recipe for Orange bread.

Currant loaf

makes two 1-lb. loaves

cooking time approximately 40 minutes

you will need:

dry mix:

1 lb. strong plain flour
1 oz. sugar
1 teaspoon salt

yeast liquid:

blend 1 oz. fresh yeast in ½ pint milk and water

or dissolve 1 teaspoon sugar in ½ pint warm (110°F. milk and water. Sprinkle on 1 level tablespoon dried yeast. Leave until frothy (about 10 minutes)

additional ingredients:

1 oz. margarine
4 oz. washed currants

1 Mix flour, sugar and salt, rub in margarine and mix in currants. Add yeast liquid and work to a firm dough, adding extra flour if needed, until the dough leaves the bowl clean.
2 Turn on to a lightly floured board and knead by stretching and folding until the dough is smooth and elastic.
3 Divide in two, flatten each piece and roll up like a Swiss roll to fit two greased 1-lb. loaf tins.
4 Place in oiled polythene bags and allow dough to rise to top of the tins.
5 Bake on middle shelf of oven at 425°F.—Gas Mark 7 for 40 - 45 minutes.
6 Brush tops of hot loaves with wet brush dipped in honey.
7 Cool on a wire tray.

Cheese loaf

cooking time 45 minutes

you will need:

dry mix:

1 lb. strong plain flour
2 level teaspoons salt and pepper
1 level teaspoon mustard
4 - 6 oz. finely grated Cheddar cheese for additional flavour

yeast liquid:

blend ½ oz. fresh yeast in ½ pint water

or dissolve 1 teaspoon sugar in ½ pint warm (110°F.) water and sprinkle 1 level teaspoon dried yeast on top. Leave until frothy (about 10 minutes)

1 Mix flour and seasoning, followed by cheese, retaining a little for the tops. Add yeast liquid and mix to a firm dough (adding more flour if necessary) that leaves the bowl clean. Turn on to a lightly floured board and knead by pulling and stretching the dough until it feels firm and elastic and no longer sticky—about 10 minutes.
2 Put the dough to rise inside an oiled polythene bag, lightly tied, or a large greased pan or plastic storage jar with lid, until it doubles in size, and springs back when pressed lightly with a floured finger.
3 When risen, turn on to a board. Knead lightly and divide into two equal pieces. Flatten each piece firmly with the knuckles to knock out the air bubbles and shape by folding in three or rolling up like a Swiss roll, tuck in the ends. The finally moulded piece should exactly fit the greased 1-lb. tins. For alternative shapes see opposite page.
4 Put the loaf tins inside oiled polythene bags and leave until the dough rises to the tops of the tins.
5 Sprinkle grated cheese on top and bake the loaves at 380°F.—Gas Mark 5 for 45 minutes. Care should be taken not to overbake.
6 Cool on a wire tray.

Variations

Cheese and celery loaf

Sprinkle 1 oz. grated cheese mixed with 1 teaspoon celery salt on top of the loaves before baking.

Cheese rolls

Divide the risen dough into 12 equal pieces and roll each piece to a ball using the palm of one hand. Press down hard at first then ease up. This is best done on an unfloured board with a litle flour on palm of one hand only. Place rolls on floured tin, rise inside polythene bag, sprinkle with cheese and bake 380°F.—Gas Mark 5, towards top of oven, for about 20 minutes.

Sandwich butters

Anchovy butter

you will need:

5 - 6 anchovy fillets
2 oz. butter
lemon juice
cochineal (optional)

1 Wash the anchovies to remove some of the salt, then pat them dry.
2 Pound well with the butter and a squeeze of lemon juice and then rub through a fine sieve.
3 Add a few drops of pink colouring.

Devilled butter

you will need:

2 oz. butter
1 level teaspoon curry powder
squeeze lemon juice
pinch white pepper
small pinch cayenne pepper

1 Beat all the ingredients together until well blended.

Green butter

you will need:

1 oz. watercress
2 oz. butter
salt
cayenne pepper

1 Wash the watercress and remove the stalks.
2 Chop very finely, then mix with the butter and beat well together.
3 Add salt and cayenne pepper to taste.

Ham butter

you will need:

2 oz. lean cooked ham or bacon
2 oz. butter
¼ level teaspoon made mustard

1 Chop the ham, put it through a mincer and then through a sieve.
2 Add the butter and mustard and beat well together.

Chutney butter

you will need:

2 oz. butter
2 oz. tomato or apple chutney
squeeze lemon juice

1 Mix all the ingredients together and work with a wooden spoon until smooth and well blended.

Piquant butter

you will need:

2 oz. butter
1 teaspoon made mustard
½ level teaspoon curry powder
1 dessertspoon lemon juice
pinch grated lemon rind

1 Mix all the ingredients together and work with a wooden spoon till well blended.

Sauces

White sauce

cooking time 10 minutes

you will need:

1 oz. butter
1 oz. flour
½ pint milk
seasoning

1 Melt the butter, stir in the flour using a wooden spoon.
2 Cook over a gentle heat for 3 minutes without browning, stirring throughout.
3 Remove from heat and gradually stir in half the milk, stir hard until well blended.
4 Return to heat, cook slowly until sauce thickens, stirring.
5 Gradually add remaining liquid.
6 Bring to boil, season with salt and pepper. Allow to boil for 2 - 3 minutes, stirring throughout.

Note

This is a thick or coating sauce, used for cauliflower cheese, filling flans and baked casserole dishes.
For a thin or pouring sauce, use ½ oz. butter and ½ oz. flour. The amount of milk and method are the same.

Variation

Cheese sauce

To ½ pint white sauce add 2 heaped tablespoons grated cheese, a little mustard, a little salt and a pinch of cayenne pepper. Add the cheese when the sauce is at boiling point, mix in well, but do not allow the sauce to boil again.

Sauce tartare

you will need:

2 teaspoons chopped capers
2 teaspoons chopped gherkins
1 teaspoon chopped parsley
½ teaspoon chopped tarragon
½ teaspoon chopped chervil
½ pint mayonnaise (see page 79)

1 Stir the chopped capers, gherkins and herbs into the mayonnaise. Use as required.

Parsley sauce

cooking time 10 minutes

you will need:

½ oz. butter
½ oz. cornflour
½ pint milk
salt and pepper
1 tablespoon parsley, finely chopped

1 Melt the butter over a low heat.
2 Add cornflour, blend well in with a wooden spoon.
3 Remove pan from heat, pour in milk, stir well.
4 Return pan to heat, bring to the boil, stirring all the time. Allow to boil steadily for 3 minutes.
5 Season to taste with salt and pepper and mix in the parsley.

Chilli sauce

cooking time 2 hours

you will need:

1 large onion
1 roasted pimento (canned)
1 large can peeled tomatoes
1 bay leaf
½ - 1 tablespoon chilli powder
1 level teaspoon salt
⅛ level teaspoon cayenne pepper
⅛ level teaspoon paprika

1 Chop onion and pimento finely.
2 Pour tomatoes into a saucepan, add onion, pimento and other seasonings.
3 Bring slowly to the boil, cover and simmer for 2 hours.
4 Remove bay leaf and leave sauce to become cold.

Bottled chilli sauce may be bought, but if you prefer to make your own, this sauce will keep in a cold place, and may be used to add a piquant flavour to meat dishes.

Horseradish cream

you will need:

2 oz. horseradish
¼ pint thick cream
salt and pepper
2 teaspoons lemon juice

1 Wash and scrape horseradish, grate finely.
2 Whisk cream until thick, season to taste with salt and pepper.

3 Stir in lemon juice and grated horseradish.
4 Chill before using if possible.

Cultured cream may be used instead of thick cream but if so, omit lemon juice.

Custard

cooking time 10 minutes

you will need:

- 3 level tablespoons custard powder
- 1 pint milk
- 2 rounded tablespoons sugar

1 Blend the custard powder with a little of the milk.
2 Bring the remaining milk to the boil.
3 Pour on to the blended custard, stirring all the time.
4 Rinse the pan with cold water, return the custard to the pan and bring to the boil over a gentle heat stirring all the time.
5 Boil for 2 - 3 minutes, add the sugar.
6 If cold custard is required, cover with a plate to prevent a skin forming.

Salad dressings

Never-fail mayonnaise

you will need:

- ¾ teaspoon sugar
- ½ teaspoon dry mustard
- ½ teaspoon salt
- pinch pepper
- 1 egg white
- 6 tablespoons corn oil
- 3 teaspoons vinegar

1 Mix sugar, mustard, salt and pepper. Blend in the egg white and beat well.
2 Continue beating, adding the corn oil a little at a time, until half is used.
3 Add 2 teaspoons vinegar, then the remaining corn oil, beating all the time.
4 Beat in the remaining vinegar.

Note

The mayonnaise can be stored if necessary in a covered jar in the refrigerator. This recipe makes about ¼ pint.

Curry mayonnaise

cooking time 5 minutes

you will need:

- 1 packet savoury white sauce mix
- ½ pint milk
- 1 level dessertspoon curry paste or powder
- ½ pint mayonnaise (see above)

1 Make up the savoury white sauce mix, with the milk, as directed on the packet.
2 Add the curry paste or powder to the sauce, and mix well.
3 Stir in the mayonnaise.
4 Leave in a cold place until required.

Tomato mayonnaise

cooking time 8 minutes

you will need:

- 1 packet tomato sauce mix
- a little less than ½ pint water
- ½ pint mayonnaise (see this page)

1 Make up the tomato sauce mix with the water, as directed on the packet. Allow to cool.
2 Stir in the mayonnaise, mix well.
3 Leave in a cold place until required.

Salad cream

you will need:

- ½ pint fairly thick white sauce (see page 78)
- 2 egg yolks
- salt and pepper
- 2 tablespoons malt vinegar
- 1 tablespoon tarragon vinegar

1 Make the sauce and remove from the heat. Stir in the beaten yolks and season to taste.
2 Cook very gently over a low heat. Do not boil.
3 Stir in the vinegars and use as required. This salad cream will keep for a short time, if it is stored in a cool place.

Cooked salad cream

cooking time 3 minutes

you will need:

- 1 level tablespoon cornflour
- 2 level teaspoons sugar
- 1 level teaspoon dry mustard
- salt, pepper and paprika, to taste
- 1 egg yolk
- 6 tablespoons corn oil
- ¼ pint sour cream
- 3 tablespoons vinegar

1 Put the cornflour, sugar, mustard and seasoning together in a saucepan.
2 Stir in the egg yolk, corn oil and cream.
3 Mix well together, boil gently for 3 minutes, stirring constantly.
4 Remove from the heat, stir in the vinegar.
5 Chill before using.

French dressing

you will need:

- 6 tablespoons corn oil
- 2 tablespoons vinegar
- pinch pepper
- pinch dry mustard
- ¼ teaspoon salt
- 1 level teaspoon sugar

1 Put all the ingredients into a small screw top jar and shake well.

Note

A little finely chopped raw onion or chopped parsley, or 2 teaspoons tomato purée may be added to the above dressing, if liked. Adjust quantities according to taste.

Pastries

Short crust pastry

you will need:

- 8 oz. flour
- pinch salt
- 2 oz. margarine
- 2 oz. lard or vegetable shortening
- cold water to mix

1 Sieve the flour and salt.
2 Chop the fat roughly and add to the flour. Rub into the flour, using the finger-tips, until the mixture resembles breadcrumbs.
3 Add cold water gradually and knead mixture lightly by hand until it works together into a firm dough.
4 Turn on to a lightly floured surface and knead lightly until smooth. Turn pastry over and roll cut as required.

Rich short crust or flan pastry

you will need:

- 8 oz. flour
- pinch salt
- 5 oz. butter
- 1 teaspoon castor sugar
- 1 beaten egg yolk
- 1 - 2 tablespoons cold water

1 Sieve flour and salt into a bowl.
2 Rub the butter lightly into the flour, using the finger-tips, until mixture resembles breadcrumbs.
3 Add sugar and egg yolk, work into the flour, adding water gradually until mixture forms a firm dough.
4 Turn on to a floured surface, knead lightly and roll out.
5 If the pastry is difficult to handle, leave in a cold place for at least 30 minutes before using.

To make a flan case:

1 Make pastry as above.
2 Roll out pastry into a circle about 2 inches larger than the flan ring.
3 Place flan ring on a baking sheet. Put the pastry over the ring and press into shape, taking care that the pastry fits well against the inside edge, but that it is not stretched.
4 Trim off surplus pastry by passing the rolling pin over the edge of the ring. Place a piece of lightly-greased paper, greased side down, in the flan case and fill the flan with uncooked rice, haricot beans or macaroni.
5 Bake in a hot oven (400°F.—Gas Mark 6) until pastry is firm (about 15 minutes). Pastry baked in this way is described as 'baked blind.' This is done to ensure a good shape. The rice etc. can be stored in a jar and used indefinitely, for this purpose.

6 Remove the filling and paper from flan. Return flan to the oven for a further 5 minutes to allow base to cook through.
7 Remove flan ring and leave flan case on a wire tray until cold.
8 Cold cooked pastry cases can be stored in an airtight tin and used as required.

Note

If a flan ring is not available, a sandwich tin may be used, but strips of paper should be placed across the inside of the tin to protrude at the edge, before the pastry is fitted. This will enable the flan case to be removed easily from the tin after cooking.

Flaky pastry

you will need:

8 oz. flour
pinch salt
6 oz. fat (butter or equal quantities of margarine and lard)
squeeze lemon juice
cold water to mix

1 Sieve flour and salt.
2 Cream the fat until soft and pliable and divide into 4 portions.
3 Rub one portion into the flour, add a squeeze of lemon juice and sufficient cold water to make a soft dough.
4 Roll the dough into an oblong. Cover two-thirds of it with another portion of fat, dabbing the fat in small pieces over the dough.
5 Fold the dough in three, starting at the bottom with the uncovered section. Bring this up to the centre of the oblong. Bring the top third down over this. Lightly press the edges together with the rolling pin.
6 Half turn the pastry to the left and roll it out into an oblong..
7 Repeat this process (5 and 6) twice, adding another portion of fat each time.
8 Fold pastry in three once more.
9 Wrap it in greaseproof paper or foil, and leave in the refrigerator or a cold place for an hour before rolling out for use.

Note

If possible, leave the pastry to 'relax' in a cool place for about 10 minutes between each rolling.

Rough puff pastry

you will need:

8 oz. flour
pinch salt
6 oz. butter or equal quantities of margarine and lard
1 teaspoon lemon juice
cold water to mix

1 Sieve the flour and salt.
2 Cut the fat into small cubes, add to the flour. Do not rub in.
3 Add lemon juice and sufficient cold water to mix to a fairly stiff dough.
4 Roll into an oblong, taking care not to stretch the pastry at the edges.
5 Fold the pastry into three. Bring the bottom end two-thirds up and the top piece down to the folded edge.
6 Seal the edges by pressing lightly with a rolling pin.
7 Half turn the pastry to the left, and roll into an oblong.
8 Repeat this process (5 and 6) twice.
9 Fold the pastry in three once more. Wrap in greaseproof paper or foil and leave in refrigerator or cold place for an hour before rolling out for use.
10 This pastry is very similar to puff pastry but is easier and quicker to make. It can be used in any recipe that requires puff or flaky pastry.

Cheese pastry

you will need:

4 oz. flour
salt
cayenne pepper
2 oz. butter
2 oz. grated Parmesan cheese
1 egg yolk
water

1 Sieve flour, salt and pepper and rub in fat very lightly with the finger-tips. Add cheese and mix well.
2 Beat the egg yolk with about 1 tablespoon water and mix into the dry ingredients to give a stiff dough. Knead lightly and use as required for biscuits etc.

Hot water crust pastry

you will need:

12 oz. flour
½ level teaspoon salt
¼ pint corn oil
¼ pint water

1. Sieve flour and salt.
2. Pour corn oil into a small saucepan, add water.
3. Heat until the mixture comes to the boil. Remove from heat, stir in the flour.
4. Mix lightly until a soft dough is formed. Knead thoroughly until smooth.
5. Use as required, while still warm.
6. Bake in a moderate oven (375°F.—Gas Mark 5).

Note

The above amount of pastry will line a loose bottomed 6-inch cake tin. This pastry is more easily handled if a loose bottomed tin is used. To prevent stock or gravy soaking into the pastry, brush the inside of the pastry with egg white.

Biscuit crust

you will need:

6 oz. digestive (sweetmeal) biscuits
3 oz. butter
about ½ oz. extra butter for preparing pie plate

1. Put the biscuits between two sheets of greaseproof paper or foil.
2. Roll with a rolling pin until the biscuits are crushed into fine crumbs.
3. Tip the crumbs into a bowl, stir in the butter and mix well.
4. Melt extra butter.
5. Brush a pie plate with melted butter.
6. Press the crumb mixture over the bottom and side of the plate.
7. Leave in a cool place to set.

This amount of crust is sufficient to line a 7 or 8-inch pie plate 1½ inches deep.

Cooking meat and eggs

Pressed beef

cooking time 3½ – 4 hours

you will need:

4 - 5 lb. pickled brisket of beef
bouquet garni (see page 66)
2 onions, peeled and stuck with two cloves
2 carrots, peeled and sliced thickly
1 turnip, peeled and sliced
2 sticks celery
water

1. Wash the meat and remove any excess fat.
2. Put into a saucepan, with the *bouquet garni* and the vegetables.
3. Cover with cold water, put the lid on the pan and simmer very gently for 3 - 4½ hours until the meat is tender.
4. Take the meat from the pan, remove any bones or gristle and press into a loaf tin or basin. Cover with a plate or saucepan and put a weight on top. Leave overnight.
5. The meat can then be turned out and glazed (see page 84) or transported in its container.

Luncheon sausage

cooking time 1½ – 2 hours

you will need:

8 oz. pork sausage meat
8 oz. beef sausage meat
2 oz. breadcrumbs
2 oz. cooked ham, chopped
salt and pepper
1 teaspoon mixed spice
pinch powdered sage
2 teaspoons chopped pickles
1 tablespoon tomato ketchup
stock

1. Mix the sausage meat, breadcrumbs and ham together.
2. Season carefully and add the spices and flavourings.
3. Mix all very well together and shape into a roll.
4. Tie in a cloth and simmer gently in stock for 1½ - 2 hours.
5. When cooked, remove from the pan and press between 2 plates with a weight on top.
6. Leave overnight, then remove the cloth and brush over with a meat glaze (see page 84).

Pork cheese

cooking time 1 hour

you will need:

- 1 lb. cold cooked pork
- 4 oz. pork fat
- 2 teaspoons chopped parsley
- 1 teaspoon grated lemon rind
- 4 leaves sage, chopped finely
- ¼ level teaspoon grated nutmeg
- salt and pepper
- little good jellied stock or gravy

1. Cut the meat into small pieces.
2. Add flavourings and season carefully.
3. Mix all well together and press into a greased basin.
4. Fill with stock.
5. Cover and cook for about 1 hour in a moderate oven (375°F.—Gas Mark 4).
6. Leave overnight to get quite cold and set.

Brawn

cooking time about 3 hours

you will need:

- 6 pigs' trotters or 1 pig's head
- 1 onion, peeled and stuck with 2 cloves
- 2 bay leaves
- 8 oz. stewing steak
- 4 - 5 sprigs parsley
- pinch mixed herbs
- salt and pepper

1. Wash the trotters or pig's head, cover with cold water and bring to boiling point, then drain and cover with clean cold water.
2. Add onion and bay leaves, cover and simmer for about 1 hour.
3. Remove the meat from the stock, cut away all bones and gristle. Chop the meat into fairly small pieces and return to stock with the stewing steak, cut into small pieces, parsley, herbs and seasoning.
4. Cover and simmer gently for about 2 hours.
5. Remove onion, bay leaves and parsley and pour into a wetted basin and leave to set.

Serve sliced as sandwich filling or accompanied by crisp salad.

Jellied flank

cooking time about 3 – 3½ hours

you will need:

- 2½ lb. flank of beef
- ½ pint water
- 1 level teaspoon salt
- 1 bay leaf
- 6 peppercorns
- stock

1. Have the meat boned and rolled by the butcher, but retain the bones.
2. Put the meat and bones into a fairly large pan, add the water, salt and flavourings.
3. Cover, bring to boiling point and simmer very gently for about 3 hours.
4. Lift out the meat, remove strings, and press the meat into a basin in which it will fit fairly tightly. Fill basin with the strained stock.
5. Cover with a plate and put a heavy weight on top, then leave overnight to get quite cold and completely set.

Jellied veal

cooking time 2½ hours

you will need:

- 2 hard-boiled eggs
- 12 oz. lean veal
- 6 oz. lean cooked ham
- 1 teaspoon chopped parsley
- 1 teaspoon grated lemon rind
- salt and pepper
- ¼ pint stock
- 1 teaspoon gelatine

1. Slice the eggs and put a few slices in the bottom of a round tin or pudding basin.
2. Cut the veal into cubes and the ham into thin slices.
3. Arrange the meat and the remaining egg in layers and sprinkle each with the parsley, lemon rind and seasoning.
4. Dissolve the gelatine in the stock, and pour it over the meat. There should be enough to just cover.
5. Cover with greased paper or foil and cook for about 2½ hours in a slow oven (325°F.—Gas Mark 2).
6. Remove from the oven and add extra stock and gelatine if necessary.
7. Cover with a plate, put a weight on top and leave overnight.

Boiled bacon

cooking time — 20 minutes per lb. and 20 minutes over

you will need:

1 joint bacon	2 bay leaves
about 2 oz. demerara sugar	6 peppercorns
	dry breadcrumbs

1 Weigh the bacon and calculate the cooking time. Allow 20 minutes per pound, with 20 minutes over.
2 Cover bacon with cold water and leave for 12 hours or overnight.
3 Dry the joint and scrape with the back of a knife to remove the 'bloom.' Rub the cut surface with demerara sugar and leave to absorb the sugar for 20 minutes.
4 Put the bacon into a pan containing enough fresh cold water to cover and bring slowly to the boil (you might need to borrow a fish kettle or large preserving pan for this). Add the bay leaves and peppercorns.
5 Simmer slowly for the calculated time. Leave the bacon in the pan until cool enough to handle. Remove and peel off the dark outside skin.
6 Dust the fat surface thoroughly with dry breadcrumbs and leave until it is quite cold before carving.

Boiled ox tongue

cooking time — 30 minutes per lb. and 30 minutes over

you will need:

1 ox tongue	1 turnip
1 onion	bunch mixed herbs
1 carrot	stock

1 Wash the tongue and soak for at least 2 hours. If it is dry or hard, soak for 12 hours.
2 Place in a large pan of cold water. Bring slowly to the boil, skim and add the vegetables and herbs. Simmer gently, 30 minutes per pound and 30 minutes over.
3 When cooked, take from the pan and remove the skin carefully.
4 Place the tongue in a bowl or tin and curl tightly. Cover with stock, place a saucer or plate on top and press with a heavy weight until cold, then turn out.

Meat glaze

Make ½ pint stock using a beef or chicken cube and ½ pint boiling water. Stir in 1 envelope of gelatine. Leave in a cold place until thick and almost setting.

Spoon over or brush on to meat loaf, gelatine, etc., as required.

Scrambled eggs

1 Allow 2 eggs for 1 person.
2 Beat the eggs well. Add salt and pepper and 1 tablespoon milk for each egg.
3 Melt just enough butter to cover the bottom of the pan. Before it is hot, put in the eggs and cook slowly over a very gentle heat. A double saucepan may be used if preferred or a basin in a saucepan with boiling water half-way up the sides of the basin.
4 As the eggs set on the bottom and sides of the pan, stir the flakes off gently with a wooden spoon but avoid stirring more than is necessary to prevent eggs sticking to the pan.
5 Stir in additional ingredients if used.
6 Pile on hot buttered toast or straight on to a warm plate, or allow to become cold to use as a sandwich filling.

Note

Scrambled eggs should be served as soon as they are set, about 5 minutes, and should be soft and creamy. Unless removed from the heat at once they will go on cooking.

Additional flavourings for scrambled eggs

For every 2 eggs, add one of the following:

1 tablespoon diced, sautéed bread cubes or cooked potato with ½ teaspoon chopped chives.

1 cooked chicken liver, finely chopped and fried with chopped bacon.

2 tablespoons chopped cooked ham, tongue or chicken.

2 tablespoons flaked cooked fish.

2 oz. chopped cooked mushrooms.

1 tablespoon chopped parsley and chives.

1½ oz. grated cheese.

2 - 3 slices liver sausage, chopped.

2 sliced cooked sausages or frankfurters.

Poached eggs

1. Use a shallow pan containing enough water to cover the eggs by 1 inch.
2. Bring water to boil, reduce to simmering.
3. Break egg into a cup, stir water then quickly slip egg in.
4. Simmer for 3 - 5 minutes, depending on firmness wanted. Do not allow water to boil or egg will be tough.
5. Remove egg with a perforated spoon. Allow it to drain, serve on a slice of hot buttered toast or on bread toasted on one side only and topped with one of the following:
   Cooked chopped spinach, coated with cheese sauce (see page 78), browned under grill if liked.
   Rice, served with tomato or curry mayonnaise (see page 79).
   Risotto, served with tomato sauce.
   Sweet corn niblets with tomato sauce.
   Spaghetti.
   Toast covered with a thin slice of cheese and grilled.
   Toast topped with mushrooms, fried in butter.
   Toast topped with a slice of ham or cooked bacon.
   Toast topped with baked beans, fried with a little chopped onion, or with curried beans.

Creams and icings

Butter cream

you will need:

6 - 8 oz. icing sugar
4 oz. butter
vanilla essence

1. Sieve the icing sugar.
2. Beat butter with a wooden spoon or spatula until soft.
3. Beat icing sugar into the butter, adding a few drops of essence.
   The amount of icing sugar needed will depend on the consistency of the cream required.

Variations

Orange or lemon butter cream

Add finely-grated lemon or orange rind and juice to taste to the creamed butter and sugar. Beat hard to prevent curdling.

Walnut butter cream

Add 2 tablespoons finely chopped walnuts to creamed butter and sugar and mix in thoroughly.

Almond butter cream

Add 2 tablespoons finely chopped toasted almonds to creamed butter and sugar.

Coffee butter cream

Make as basic butter cream, adding the vanilla essence and 2 teaspoons coffee essence.

Mocha butter cream

Make as coffee butter cream, adding 2 oz. melted chocolate as well as the coffee essence.

Chocolate butter cream

Melt a 2 oz. bar plain chocolate. Beat 2 oz. butter until soft. Blend in the melted chocolate and 3 oz. sieved icing sugar.

Glacé icing

you will need:

8 oz. icing sugar
2 - 3 tablespoons warm water
flavouring and colouring as liked

1. Sieve the icing sugar into a bowl, using a wooden spoon to press sugar through sieve if necessary.
2. Add water gradually, beating well until icing is smooth and glossy and of a good coating consistency, i.e. will coat the back of a spoon.
3. Add flavouring and colouring and blend well into the mixture.
   If icing is required only for the top of the cake, it should be slightly thicker so it can be spread out smoothly and kept to the edge.

Variations

Lemon or orange glacé icing

Make as above, using 2 tablespoons lemon juice or orange juice instead of water and add 2 - 3 drops orange or lemon colouring.

Coffee glacé icing

Make as above, reducing the amount of water by 2 teaspoons and using 2 teaspoons coffee essence.

Chocolate glacé icing

Melt 2 oz. plain chocolate in a small bowl over a pan of hot water. Blend in 4 oz. sieved icing sugar and 1 tablespoon water. For extra gloss, add 2 - 3 drops oil.

Wrapping and Packing Sandwiches and Picnic Meals

Sandwiches and more adventurous packed meals have become very much part of our lives, whether for the children's school lunch, as a time and money-saving meal to take to work or for a picnic on a relaxing day out.

Whatever the reason for preparing a packed meal, the modern and attractive, well-designed containers, as well as materials like kitchen foil and cling film, not only enable us to transport the meal without any spoilage but also to keep the food looking as attractive and tasting as fresh as when it was first packed.

Sandwiches and salads can be prepared several hours in advance, or on the evening before, and stored in an airtight container in the refrigerator. This helps to avoid any last minute panic in the morning! However, there are a few basic rules to remember when preparing sandwiches or filled rolls well in advance:

1 Do not use sliced tomatoes, cucumber, beetroot or lettuce as they will make the bread soggy and unappetising. Sandwiches containing these ingredients should be prepared only an hour or so before serving, or even later if possible.

2 Fillings that might spoil the bread can still be made up in advance and stored in small airtight containers in the refrigerator; for example, fish and tomato filling or crab and cucumber.

3 Fillings such as devilled egg and ham, tuna and capers, liver sausage and pickle are ideal for using in sandwiches prepared hours in advance.

4 Salads and salad vegetables can also be stored well and attractively in airtight picnic containers. Carrot and celery sticks, lettuce leaves, radishes and mixed salads such as coleslaw not only make a crisp and colourful accompaniment to any simple packed meal, but they are also a good source of minerals and vitamins which ensure a well-balanced diet.

5 Salad dressings can be made up in advance and stored in small tightly sealed containers. Never add the dressing to the salad hours in advance, or some of the ingredients (particularly lettuce) will loose their crispness and refreshing taste. Make sure that you pour the dressing into a tightly sealed container, and take it with you to add to the salad just before eating.

Some Useful Containers

Modern containers are designed not only to be food saving but also space saving. They now come in a variety of shapes and sizes from the smallest square box, oval platters and tall oblong containers, to large round cake storers. Most designs allow the canisters to be stacked when not in use. In addition, for maximum flexibility, the majority of these containers are both freezer and dishwasher proof.

1 Lunch Boxes

There are a great many different types and designs of lunch box available, from a small child's tuck box to a substantial adult's lunch box. There are even lunch boxes with removable dividers to separate the individual food items: so your first course of sardine sandwiches won't necessarily have to flavour the gingerbread, and the salad won't make a meat pie soggy. Most of these containers are also light and neat enough to fit into a school bag or slim brief case.

Packed meals need not be bulky and fattening, a nice light salad, with a slice or two of crispbread and piece of fruit, is ideal for the slimmer who wants to resist the temptation of a hamburger and chips for lunch!

2 Drink Containers

Drinks are a very important part of packed meals and there is no shortage of containers to choose from — numerous cups, beakers, mugs and serving jugs with tight-fitting lids to avoid any spillages. For very cold drinks or hot winter soups there are also beautifully designed vacuum flasks — many of them unbreakable.

3 Picnic Containers

For a large family picnic, it is now possible to transport an entire meal with the help of specially designed containers. You can prepare a whole range of food in advance, then just nip off to your favourite picnic spot and relax for the rest of the day. For a change, why not prepare a cold buffet meal? Buy or make veal and ham pies, a salmon mousse ring, a selection of salads, rice or new potatoes, or any other vegetables of your choice. This mouth-watering feast can be followed by a sumptuous upside-down trifle, fruit salad or even peach melba. There are some containers on the market with lids that can be used as a plate, which saves time, space and washing up.

4 Everyday Storage Containers

Many unbreakable containers can serve a dual purpose, when they are not in use for picnics or packed meals they make excellent general storage containers — whether in the cupboard, refrigerator or freezer. Cakes and biscuits keep fresher and crisper, cold meats and bacon keep better in the refrigerator, and some soups keep for months in the freezer.

By making use of the whole range of containers for a number of different purposes you save space and money.

Index

C

D

E

F

G

H

I

J

K

L

M

N

O

P

Q

R

S

V

W